THE STORY OF THE CELTIC

W. MALEY

THE STORY OF
THE CELTIC

W. MALEY

DESERT ISLAND BOOKS

First published in 1939

This facsimile edition published
in 1996 by
DESERT ISLAND BOOKS
34 Hamlet Court Road, Westcliff-on-Sea, Essex SS0 7LX
United Kingdom

British Library Cataloguing-in-Publication Data:
A catalogue record for this book is available from the British Library.

ISBN   1-874287-15-5

Printed in Great Britain
by
Redwood Books, Trowbridge, Wiltshire

Publisher's note:
The first edition of this book was published
in Crown size (180 x 120 mm).
This edition is published in Demy-Octavo (216 x 138 mm).
The text has been magnified by 7½ per cent

PREFACE

THE inside story of any enterprise is invariably interesting, but when that enterprise assumes proportions greatly in excess of those anticipated by its promoters the telling of it cannot fail to appeal.

The history of the Celtic Club must accordingly be eagerly read, as it is unique in that, from a very humble beginning, the Club in its first year created a standard which I make bold to say has not only been maintained but increased, to the benefit of football throughout the country.

The great appeal of this history lies, however, in the fact that the Author does not require to depend on the information and experience of others in the carrying out of his task. The story must be regarded as almost a personal one, as he was in a manner of speaking present at the birth of the Club, played a prominent part in nursing it through its infancy, steered it through its period of adolescence, and still remains at the helm to guide it through the many difficulties which from time to time beset its path.

Mr. William Maley in the history of the Celtic makes no effort to clothe his story with fine words and high-sounding phrases. He gives it in plain language and endeavours—very successfully in my opinion—to trace the progress of the Club through the years.

The tale of its early struggles against antipathy, distrust and jealousy is told without any bitterness, although during the early days there was much to contend with.

Not only friends of the Celtic but lovers of the game generally are indebted to Mr. Maley for his " history ". It reveals many things of which even I, who have been a director for thirty-three years, was unaware.

No other person could have attempted the task which Mr. Maley has so successfully accomplished, and I commend it to the public with the utmost confidence and the greatest pleasure.

31st July, 1939.

CONTENTS

LIST OF PLATES

LIST OF PLATES

The Celtic Club

IN writing the story of the Celtic as I have seen it, I have no intention of making a detailed history of the Club. The doings of the Celtic are well known to all followers of the game.

In this book I will endeavour to recount the rise of the Club with the names, &c., of those responsible in the main for its birth.

In the book will be found photographs and descriptive notes of the leading officials and players over the years, which will, I am sure, be welcomed by the readers.

Further, in addition to the Scroll of Honour of Cups and Championships won, there will be a short description of the greatest games of the Club over its fifty years.

A short description of the Club's Jubilee Celebrations will also be given, in addition to one or two other odd features which will, I hope, make up a book to be treasured by all who love the Celtic Club.

When telling the story of the rise of the Celtic, I think I can claim that it is the most wonderful story of all the Club formations that have been disclosed.

The story starts with the success of the Edinburgh Hibs, who were formed in 1872 and who found in their early days the same press antagonism which at first threatened to swamp Celtic, but faded away before a resolute body of men who plainly had come to stay.

The Hibs, up till the coming of Celtic, had had a very fine life, and in their short existence had won all the Eastern honours, and in 1887 were the first team to take the Scottish Cup to " Fair Edina ".

Their team was mostly made up of Western players recruited by the energetic Hibs from teams such as Lugar Boswell, Cowlairs, Vale of Leven and Airdrie.

The Scottish Cup victory came as a great pride to their West of Scotland supporters, who, whenever the Hibs played in the West, supported them in great numbers.

The Renton, who were in their prime in those years, had played a charity game in Glasgow with the Hibs for the benefit of the Poor Children's Dinner-table of the East End, with very beneficial results to the energetic committee who promoted the match.

When the Hibs won the Scottish Cup they were fêted by their Glasgow supporters, who drove them to St. Mary's Hall, East Rose St., and gave them a dinner and later presented them with mementoes of their great deed.

All this had inspired the Glasgow Irishmen's ambition to run a team in Glasgow, then growing great with additions to the resident Irish through the big city works of drainage, &c., for which the Irish labourer proved himself so useful.

From the three Catholic Parishes of St. Andrew's, St. Mary's and St. Alphonsus there emanated a desire to put the matter to the test, and several meetings were held to decide what course of action should be taken to put the proposed Club right on the way. As in all things

Irish, at that time, jealousies arose and various good men drew out rather than submit to being shoved aside by the more pushing sort always to be found.

St. Mary's representatives, with the greatest enthusiasm, eventually forced matters to an issue, and at a big meeting held in St. Mary's Hall it was decided to proceed with the formation of the Club and to look for the necessary ground.

The St. Andrew's representatives felt themselves sidetracked and withdrew from the project, although several of their best folks stuck to their guns and helped the project along. A famous family in those days was the Macreadies, " Old Dominic " of that ilk having a very popular bar in Saltmarket, where all the youth of Donegal came for a job when they landed off the " palatial " boats, which in those days did alike for human beings and cattle. Three of the Macreadies stuck to the new venture, and John Macreadie acted on committee for three years.

The Rector of St. Mary's Parish in those days was the Revd. Donald Carmichael, who, like his contemporary the famous Fr. Munro of St. Andrew's Cathedral of happy memory, had no time for football and its following. He had, however, the saving grace of letting things take their course to see how matters would work out. His curates were very enthusiastic in the work and helped the cause along with their very best efforts.

The Archbishop of Glasgow of that day, Archbishop Eyre, gave his patronage to the good work, which stated that the Club was formed for the purpose of obtaining funds for the feeding of the poor children of the East

End, of which in those days there was a very large number.

The first Honorary President of the Club was Dr. John Conway, a local M.D., and his President was John Glass, a working joiner to whom, in my estimation, the Club owes its existence, as he never shirked from that time till the day of his death to further the project which to him appealed as his life work.

Behind those two men came the other great inspirer in the good work, Bro. Walfrid, a Marist Brother then at the head of this Teaching Order in Glasgow. Born in Ballymote, Co. Sligo, 18th May, 1840, by name Andrew Kerins, he laboured as a Marist Brother for fifty-one years and died in 1915 and is buried in St. Joseph's College, Dumfries. He was the most enthusiastic Celt who ever lived. It was to him that the Club owes its name, as he managed to get the new committee to adopt it as against a strong proposal to call the Club the Glasgow Hibernians.

To tell the real story of the rise of the Celtic, I must inevitably bring in a little of my own life story, although of course I was not on the scene when those great minds of the East End and St. Andrew's parishes decided they would make still another effort to build a Catholic Club in Glasgow on the lines of the never-to-be-forgotten Hibernians of Edinburgh of those far-away days.

After a few meetings in 1887 John Glass, Bro. Walfrid and Pat, or Tailor Welsh, as he was familiarly known in St. Mary's Parish, Abercromby St., Glasgow, came out to my home in Cathcart to interview Tom, my brother, who was then a very fine forward and had played quite a lot for Partick Thistle, Third Lanark and Hibernians. It was felt that if his services could be secured they would have the start of team building which was so necessary for the Club's success. Tom was not at home, and I arranged to get him to meet the party in Glasgow to hear their proposals. Bro. Walfrid said to me, " Why don't you come with him." I replied that I was only a second-rater and had almost decided to give up the game for cross-country running. He persuaded me to come in with Tom, and when Tom decided to join up my name went down too, and so I was at once initiated into the wonderful scheme of things that this committee of men, with no football knowledge at all, had built up, and which their tremendous enthusiasm eventually brought to fruition.

I was young, strong, with plenty of speed and had a happy knack of quickly absorbing advice or tuition, and over the fifty years of my wanderings for this great Club I have learned much which has, thank God, made me as good as my neighbour, and I have, with dignity and ability, been able to uphold the name of the Celtic which is so dear to me both on and off the field.

It is but natural that in the story I may overlook some good fellow who may have in his day had as much Celtic enthusiasm as I have had, but feel sure he will forgive me and lay the blame on the memory which has stood the stress of long years.

In the very early days of this Club, when money was very scarce, one cannot tell how much it owed to the hard work of the men who voluntarily built the old ground, and later the new ground to which we moved after our practical eviction. Again the same remark applies to the good fellows who acted as gatemen or cashtakers in the days when every penny was required to keep the Club's head above water, and to disappoint the many unfriends we had in those days who wished to see the Club a failure like the other few efforts of previous years, when attempts had been made to form a Glasgow Hibernian Club on the lines of the then great Edinburgh Club.

The Committee formed to carry through the great work was as follows, viz.:—

Hon. President
Dr. John Conway

President
John Glass

Treasurer	*Secretary*	*Match Secretary*
Hugh Darroch	John O'Hara	William Maley

Committee

J. M. Nelis, Joseph Shaughnessy, M. Cairns, J. H. McLaughlin, W. McKillop, T. E. Maley, Daniel Malloy, John McDonald, Joseph McGrory, David Meikleham and P. Welsh.

Of that lot only Mr. J. M. Nelis and myself are now alive.

The formation of the new Committee caused a lot of heartburnings amongst the members, and even then many retired from their membership, which at that time was about 400.

The following circular was issued in January, 1888, asking for financial assistance, which came along, but not in the amount that was desired.

Circular

CELTIC FOOTBALL AND ATHLETIC CLUB
CELTIC PARK, PARKHEAD
(Corner of Dalmarnock and Janefield Streets)

Patrons

His Grace the Archbishop of Glasgow and the Clergy of St. Mary's, Sacred Heart, and St. Michael's Missions, and the principal Catholic laymen of the East End.

The above Club was formed in November, 1887, by a number of the Catholics of the East End of the City.

The main object of the Club is to supply the East End conferences of the St. Vincent De Paul Society with funds for the maintenance of the " Dinner Tables " of our needy children in the Missions of St Mary's, Sacred Heart, and St. Michael's. Many cases of sheer poverty are left unaided through lack of means. It is therefore with this principal object that we have set afloat the " Celtic ", and we invite you as one of our every-ready friends to assist in putting our new Park in proper working order for the coming football season.

We have already several of the leading Catholic football players of the West of Scotland on our membership list. They have most thoughtfully offered to assist in the good work.

We are fully aware that the " élite " of football players belong to this City and suburbs, and we know that from there we can select a team which will be able to do credit to the Catholics of the West of Scotland as the Hibernians have been doing in the East.

Again there is also the desire to have a large recreation

ground where our Catholic young men will be able to enjoy the various sports which will build them up physically, and we feel sure we will have many supporters with us in this laudable object.

Any subscriptions may be handed to any of the Clergy of the three Missions or to the President, Mr. John Glass, 60 Marlborough Street, Glasgow, Dr. John Conway, 14 Abercromby Street, Glasgow, or to J. O'Hara, 77 East Rose Street, Glasgow, or to any member of the Committee, and same will be gratefully acknowledged in course.

The following subscriptions have already been received, viz.:

His Grace the Archbishop	20s.
Very Revd. Canon Carmichael	20s.
Revd. F. J. Hughes	20s.
Revd. A. Beyaert	20s.
Revd. A. Vanderhyde	20s.
Dr. John Conway	20s.
Mr. John Higney	20s.
Mr. James Doyle	20s.
Mr. Arthur McHugh	20s.
Mr. Thos. McCormick	20s.
Mr. Henry Aylmer	20s.
Mr. Michael Aylmer	20s.
Mr. George Hughes	20s.
Mr. Daniel Hughes	20s.
Mr. James Quillan	20s.
Mr. James McQuillan	20s.
Mr. James McConnell	20s.
Mr. John McGallegley	20s.
Mr. John Clancy	20s.
Mr. Francis Henry	20s.
Mr. John Conway	20s.
Mr. James Conway	20s.
Mr. E. Williamson	20s.
Mr. Andrew Bryan	20s.

Mr. Jos. A. Foy	20s.
Mrs. Flynn	20s.
The Granite House	10s. 6d.
Mr. John Brown	10s. 6d.
Mr. John Brien	10s. 6d.
Mr. Hugh Darroch	10s. 6d.
Mr. P. Donegan	10s. 6d.
Mr. Hugh Swan	10s. 6d.
Mr. Patrick Gaffney	10s. 6d.
Mr. James Hughes	10s. 6d.
Mr. James McCann	10s. 6d.
Mr. P. McCulloch	10s. 6d.
Mr. Owen Aylmer	10s. 6d.
Mr. Louis Mackenzie	10s. 6d.
Mr. John Blair	10s.
Mr. Edward Mooney	10s.
Mr. Charles Stewart	10s.
Mr. Wm. Stewart	10s.
A Friend	10s.
A Friend	10s.
Mr. Young	10s.

A large number of subscriptions were later acknowledged, among these being one from Mr. R. F. Barr of the firm now known as A. G. Barr & Co., Ltd., the well-known aerated water manufacturers.

The period of the start of the Club was what is now known as the day of the paid amateur. England had declared for professionalism in 1888, but the S.F.A., with that stupidity which has often marked her actions, muddled along sternly set against what a leading writer said would be the *utter ruin of the game*. If he were alive to-day to see what professionalism had done for it, what would he say?

The leading Glasgow clubs, with of course the one exception, Queen's Park, were all paid amateurs, and both Hearts and Hibs had benefited from the many good lads they brought from the West at the sight of the gold of those days.

England had an open door to the North and came and took away what she wanted, as the famous Preston North End team proved when Mr. Sudell formed what was to my mind the greatest team of all time, eight of whom were Scots who were not allowed to earn a football living at home.

Celtic accepted the opportunity, after prolonged negotiations in which the good name and character of my brother Tom, who had played for the Hibs in Edinburgh, proved a big asset. He was a schoolmaster and a man of fine appearance and character. He was well thought of by the men he played with, and so when he cast his lot in with the Celtic the men in the East he wanted soon came along. McLaren, that great half-back; Groves, the dashing forward; McKeown, the wandering Celt; Gallacher, a Johnstone man but playing for the Hibs; Dunbar of Busby; and Coleman of Cathcart all gave their word to play for the new Club.

James Kelly and Neilly McCallum of Renton, then at the top of the tree in football, had promised to play for the Hibs, but when the new Club appeared it was soon settled and they joined the great majority and came over to Celtic.

We had a spate of goalkeepers, the first one to play for us being Michael Dolan of Drumpellier, Coatbridge, although his stay with us was short. Our first regular goalkeeper was W. Dunning from Johnstone, but he only served a few months. Then we had John Kelly from Newton Mearns, who played in the famous Snow Final for us. He left us after four months of good service, but he can be reckoned as one of the first year's team which brought honour and credit to the name of our Club.

After those goalkeepers we played Tobin and McLaughlin, and in 1890 captured James Bell of Mauchline, who had played for Dumbarton, but he only remained a year with us, when he too was superseded by Tom Duff from Cowlairs. Followed Joe Cullen from the Benburb junior team, who in turn gave way to Dan McArthur, whom I reckon the first of our real star goalkeepers.

The first game the Celtic played officially was at Celtic Park on 29th May, 1888, when the following team sported the new Celtic colours against Rangers in a friendly game, Celtic winning by 5 to 2.

Goal
Michael Dolan (Drumpellier)

Right back	*Left back*
Eddie Pearson	J McLaughlin
(Carfin)	(Govan Whitefield)

Right half-back	*Centre half-back*	*Left half-back*
William Maley	James Kelly	Phil Murray
(Cathcart)	(Renton)	(Blantyre)

Forwards
O.R., Neil McCallum (Renton). I.R., T. E. Maley (Cathcart). Centre, John Madden (Dumbarton). I.L., M. Dunbar (Busby). O.L., H. Gorevin (Govan Hibs).

RANGERS:

Goal

Nicol

Right back   *Left back*
McIntyre   Muir

Right half-back *Centre half-back* *Left half-back*
McPherson   McFarlane   Meikle

Forwards

O.R., Robb. *I.R.*, McLaren. *Centre*, McKenzie. *I.L.*,
Souter. *O.L.*, Wilson

REFEREE: Mr. McFadden
                 (*Edinburgh Hibernians*)

It is a marvellous thing to look back on this game
with its intensive rivalry of that day, and to realize that
fifty years afterwards the two clubs should be the greatest
attraction there is in not only Scottish but British football
to-day.

The colours Celtic wore that day were white shirts
with a green collar and a Celtic Cross in red and green
on the left breast. These were presented to the Club
by Penman Bros., then the big drapers and clothiers at
Bridgeton Cross.

The first Committee was composed of men with no
football or athletic knowledge excepting the brothers
Maley; J. H. McLaughlin played cricket in a small way,
whilst Mr. John McDonald of Springburn was a follower
of Powderhall professional foot-running.

The personality of John Glass in those days was the
cause of many lads joining the Celts. Like Father

O'Flynn, "he had a wonderful way wid him". He was a great Irishman, ever ready to stand up for his rights, and later did much politically for the cause so dear to him. Those were not the days of written agreements, and John Glass's word was always as good as any bond.

Pride of place must always be given to Celtic's first season, not by reason of its being its first year, but because of the circumstances of its formation and the unique circumstances which it created. It is correct to say that the men who set the machinery in motion were absolute novices so far as football knowledge, &c., was concerned, and it is equally correct to say that, from the formation of the Association and the inception of the Cup to the present day, no Club has ever made such a sensational debut and continued in the limelight as Celtic has done.

" Knowing " novices were those early Celts. They enlisted men who knew and played the game—a most desirable asset in producing the necessary team spirit.

The original ground of the Club is now occupied by the works of A. G. Barr & Coy. at Parkhead. It was small, but in those days seemed the last word to the pioneers of the Club. It was held on a rent of £50 per year and was bounded on the west by the walls of Janefield Cemetery.

The ground was built with a stand, underneath which were the dressing-rooms for two teams, with shower baths, also small office and trainer's room and store and referee's room.

The ground was opened in May, 1888, by a match

between Hibs and Cowlairs, at which the attendance was about 5000.

With the work of the ground now off their minds, the Committee settled down properly to form their team, and soon they received many offers from players all over the country to join the new Celtic. They decided, however, that nothing short of a first-class team would do to launch the new venture on the Scottish football arena.

The ground being held on a yearly basis, trouble came when 1892 brought an old affliction to Irishmen, " The Landlord ". Rack-renting brought about a change of field. A rent raised after three short years' occupancy from £50 to £500 a year proved the mettle of the new Celtic.

At one time it was thought to go out to Possilpark or Springburn, but as the Cowlairs had sort of official rights to the northern district the idea was abandoned. When one sees the extension of the city, Possilpark would have been a great spot for the Celts, where with very cheap ground in those days a wonderful erection might have been there now as the Celtic stadium.

A seemingly impossible site, actually a quarry hole between the old ground and London Road, was converted quickly into a palatial enclosure, and it looked, as one smart chap said, " Like leaving the graveyard to enter Paradise ". That title, seized on by a pressman, clung to the present ground for many years.

The lessons learned and the experience gained on the old monument to the loyalty and fidelity of pioneers of the Club who gave their labours to construct it were not lost. A new ground much in advance of anything yet seen in Scotland marked the opening of the new Celtic Park, with its two splendid tracks for foot-running and cycling, the latter in later years remodelled to a cement surface housing a world's championship, which is still remembered by old-timers.

The Club purchased the ground in time from Lord Newlands, and although it is not as large as either Hampden or Ibrox, it can hold comfortably 70,000 and has covered accommodation at all times for 18,000 people, which is better than any other club outside these two enclosures.

The first sod, of real Irish shamrocks, of the new ground of 1892 was laid by the famous Irish Patriot, Michael Davitt, and to commemorate the occasion a poem appeared in one of the Catholic papers of that day as follows:

On alien soil like yourself I am here;
I'll take root and flourish, of that never fear,
And though I'll be crossed sore and oft by the foes
You'll find me as hardy as Thistle or Rose.
If model is needed on your own pitch you will have it,
Let your play honour me and my friend Michael Davitt.

A souvenir hunter or vandal carried off that Donegal sod, so its shamrocks never bloomed, but what befell the one who removed the turf no man knoweth.

He carried, however, for ever the weight of the poet's wrath, as when it became known the following verse was published:

The curse of Cromwell blast the hand that stole the sod that
     Michael cut;
May all his praties turn to sand—the crawling, thieving scut.
That precious site of Irish soil with verdant shamrocks
     overgrown
Was token of a glorious soil more fitting far than fretted stone.
Again I say, may Heaven blight that envious, soulless knave;
May all his sunshine be like night and the sod rest heavy on
     his grave.

Like all things Irish, the new Club found there was
always contention and plenty of room for argument
amongst the new-fangled membership, and with a big
Committee of twenty duly elected by the one-man-vote
theory there was, as was the case in all the big clubs
once they started to take a prominent position, much
canvassing and wangling to get positions on the Committee.   Luckily for Celtic, the leaders, John Glass and
Bro. Walfrid, held a commanding place in the hearts
of the leading members and were able to get a Committee which, with exceptions, was after their own hearts.

At times there were serious troubles, however, and on
one occasion, through bad checking in the counting of
the votes by certain persons selected for this purpose,
we had to face a circular from a number of the members
calling for a recount, which eventually brought a new
election in which, however, there was very little change
from the first, except for the replacing of one individual.

The year 1893 brought Scotland professionalism and
with that step the whole outlook of Celtic was changed.
Previously we could depend on the best of our own particular nationality and faith to have aspirations to play

for the Club, but the lure of gold made things different, and we found that many really good men placed the cash first, and one can hardly blame them.

The insecurity of an ordinary working club was not quite sufficient for those who had to bear the worries of working the Celtic.

Various schemes were devised to put the Club on a sound business footing, but each year saw the best efforts of the real managers of the Club thwarted by the change of new men, who had neither the knowledge nor the time to keep the Club up to standard, being elected to the Committee. Again the financial question came in, and with John Glass and a few of the Committee signing overdrafts the position became acute, when it was found that certain people wanted power without any financial liability. They were quite content to leave this to others.

The matter came to a head when at a special meeting called in 1896 to consider the Club's financial position, the " Heads " stated distinctly that the Club must be put on a sound footing or else close down.

A member pooh-poohed this idea and stated he could get £500 in five minutes as a beginning of security. He was taken at his word, and next day two members of the Committee, by appointment, waited for this man to fulfil his promise. He never appeared, and at a meeting of Committee later said he was only joking. Thereafter the men who actually made our Club proceeded to put it on a real business footing. They felt the Club must expand and the only way to do so was by making it a limited company, and so Celtic became such with a capital of £10,000.

The old members had all the liabilities wiped out and each received £1 Founders share, which has since been added to by another share with 10s. paid on same out of profits.

John Glass was granted 200 £1 shares in recognition of his early work for the Club, so that the Club started with 301 Founders shares and 699 shares of £1, all subscribed for by the ultimate shareholders of the Celtic Football & Athletic Co.

At the start of the Company a temporary Board was chosen as follows: J. H. McLaughlin, M. Dunbar, T. E. Maley, J. O'Hara, J. McKay, J. Glass, M. Hughes, which, however, when the share allotment had taken place, was replaced by the following, the first duly elected Board of the new Company:

J. H. McLaughlin (*Chairman*), John Glass, John O'Hara, Michael Dunbar, John McKillop, James Kelly, James Grant. It included an entirely new name in that of Mr. James Grant, a North of Ireland man, big, strong and very plain-spoken. He in 1898 erected the Grant Stand, the first two-decker stand to be built in football.

He had the idea of having large sliding windows which could be shut when the day was wet, but the architect had overlooked the " sweating " which took place through the breaths of the spectators in the stand, and so the windows got obscured and eventually were taken away altogether. The stand was never a popular one owing to the climb up to it by four flights of stairs, and also it was on the opposite side of the field from the pavilion of those days, and Mr. Grant lost a lot of money through his enterprise and eventually sold it to the Company at a small price.

It was burned down in 1927 when being taken down to make way for the present cosy stand and pavilion.

The old Club stand on the north side of the field had of course been burned down in 1904, the day after a famous victory, and to this day it is believed it was " set off " by someone who had no love for the green-and-white brigade.

This stand had fond memories for us, as in football and also in the days of our great sports meetings it was the busy hive of the bookmakers, when one could win a thousand or two from a Celtic sprint handicap.

The year 1898 saw other changes on the ground, as in that year the World's Cycling Championships were held in Scotland (for the first and only time), and we built a cement track to meet the occasion, on which for many years the finest cyclists in the world, both pedal and motor, delighted the largest crowds which up to then had patronized sports.

Harry Martin, the dashing motor-cyclist of those days, used to thrill the crowd with his 45-mile-per-hour dashes, which then seemed wonderful. Martin was a marvellous chap, and I remember him coming north one Saturday to run for us after a spill at Northampton, where on a grass track he was somersaulted owing to a burst tyre, and had to be taken to a hospital. Nevertheless he was with us, all patched up but bruised, to do his stuff to a welcome he dearly liked to hear.

On this track, too, we once had A. E. Wills, who had just come from Paris, where he had ridden 61 miles in the hour behind a monster motor-cycle which he brought over with him. It was too powerful for our circumscribed track, and he could not let it out in case he might crash over the iron railings which we had then round the track by order of the Scottish Football Association for protection in international games.

Cycling eventually killed itself by reason of the riders' loafing tactics, which did not suit the public, and in order to enlarge our standing accommodation the cycle track was taken away and banking installed, which has held to the present day; but oftentimes I wish I could bring back those days with their thrilling cycling finishes with a Vogt, Killachy, McLaren, Flynn, Zimmerman, Arend, Bourillon, O'Neill, Barden, and a host of others making the spectators rise in their enthusiasm.

From the change over to Limited Liability position in 1898 the Club gradually settled into a real business state, and much good work was done in making Celtic Park one of the best grounds in the country.

It was a beautiful sight when on a big match or sports day a huge crowd filled up what was then the last word in terracings. The coloured cement cycling track set off the whole field and the huge Grant Stand added to the *tout ensemble*.

Celtic at that time had a great opportunity of crowding out all opposition, if they had had the foresight to see what the game was coming to. They had then the chance of taking in all the ground right down to London Road, where the big school is now, and if that had been done the present ground could have run north and south, with room for terracings equal to Hampden of to-day.

At that period, however, we had the wooden terracings, which cost a deal of money to erect and much more to maintain as against the dumps of solid earth of to-day, which, once laid down and terraced, have only to be kept in repair.

Celtic Park, however, had its day as regards International fame, and can lay claim to be the first club to build for Internationals. We can always look back with pride to some of the great games which were played there, particularly the famous Rosebery International of 1900, in which Scotland gave England one of the greatest defeats of the very long series by football of the very highest standard.

During the War, too, the ground served a great purpose in football games and sports for the great cause of charity, and there, too, was seen a baseball game between teams from the American navy, who were at the time lying at the Tail of the Bank.

At one of these sports also it will be remembered there was a touch of war, as many wounded soldiers, preparatory to returning to the trenches, gave a display of trench warfare. They erected temporary dummy trenches which were defended and attacked with all sorts of harmless bombs, which made a great noise but caused no damage; and the soldiers put great zest into their display, which was inaugurated by the explosion of a land mine in the centre of Celtic Park, which, prompt to " pip emma ", blew up to start the mimic war, an item greatly enjoyed by the huge crowd assembled.

Again it was on Celtic Park that the first of these huge displays of musical drill by school children was given.

After seeing this item given in London on the Chelsea
F.C. ground, I induced the Education Authority of
Glasgow to attempt the same in Glasgow. It was a huge
success, and later on during the Coronation Festivities
it was renewed at Hampden Park with great success.

Another great day was in 1911, during the Coronation
rejoicings in London. A great parade of colonial and
home troops was held at Celtic Park, where we had
soldiers from all the British colonies and possessions,
who gave a display that must still linger in the minds of
those privileged to see it.

Celtic in their early days were always ready to purvey
for their patrons every kind of sport. Boxing was encouraged, but did not take on as expected.

Before aeroplanes became so common as they are to-
day, Celtic offered what was then the big sum of £500
to Graham White, then the doyen of airmen, to fly into
and out of their ground. Everything seemed all right
until White came down to see the ground plan. The
iron railings round the playing pitch were at once objected to, but that was a detail, and it was agreed to take
them down for the day. The steepness of the terracing
was, however, the snag which killed the engagement, as
with only a run of 150 yards he felt he could not be
certain of rising clear of the bank; and so a great attraction failed to materialize.

Our experiences in ground building were of great help
to Hampden and Ibrox when their day came, and
although Celtic Park to-day cannot compete for big
crowds with their two great friends and rivals, Celtic
Park full at some big occasion is as pretty a sight as

BRO. WALFRID, MARIST BROTHERS

M. DUNBAR

Played for Celtic team 1888 to 1891. Committeeman 1891 to 1897
Director from 1897 to 1921. Died 1921

JAMES McKAY

Acted as a Committeeman from 1888 until 1897. Was also Treasurer
from 1892 until 1897. Acted as Oversman in construction of new ground
from 1895 until 1897

JOSEPH SHAUGHNESSY

Hon President, 1892
Committee from 1888 until 1897

JAMES KELLY

Played for Celtic team from 1888 until 1897. Was a Member of the
famous Renton team of 1884–1887. Played many International games.
Acted as Committeeman in old Club and was added to Board in 1897.
Served as Chairman of Club 1909 until 1914. Died 1931

JOHN GLASS

Acted on First Committee as Vice-President until 1890 and as Chairman of Club from 1890 until 1897, when he joined Board of Limited Coy. and served until his death in 1906

1888

Top row, right to left: J. McDonald, J. Glass, D. Malloy, J. Quillan, Committeemen, and Joe Anderson, Trainer

2nd row: W. McKillop and John O'Hara, Committeemen

3rd row: M. Dunbar, W. Maley, W. Dunning, P. Gallacher, T. E. Maley, and W. Groves

Bottom row: M. McKeown, N. McCallum, J. Kelly, J. McLaren, and John Coleman

JAMES GRANT

Committee 1896 and 1897
Board of Directors from 1897 until death in 1914

can be seen on any ground in Britain, with its cosy and symmetrical design of ground and stands.

In 1929 when the Club, forced by the fires in the Grant Stand and pavilion, had to rebuild entirely, they faced a very large expenditure, and to their credit soon wiped that out. The new stand, &c., cost almost £35,000, and this was paid in five years, a testimony surely to the business-like methods of the Board, who in that period brought in some very big transfer fees without weakening to any extent their team.

In the pages to follow will be found much information of great interest to our readers.

Stories of the greatest games of the Club, with photographs of several of its greatest players and little sketches of their lives, will be given.

The list of the Board since the formation of the Club into a Limited Company is also given, and it will be interesting to see how little real change there has been for many years. Of course all the earliest pioneers have gone, with the exception of myself, but it will surprise many to read of the years of service that have been put in for the Club by Mr. Tom Colgan and Mr. Tom White, both of whom are still fit and well to continue their good work for Celtic.

The subject of which has been the best Celtic team in the fifty years of its existence can easily be answered by a reference to the results tables over the years.

The period between 1904 until 1910 found the Celts with a side which has never been equalled in Scottish football, and which has placed its name irrevocably on the history of the game.

They won the League Flag for six successive years, and have left to the future managements a beautiful silver shield presented to the Club by the Scottish Football League to commemorate their wonderful feat. This feat was achieved by first-class football, and even to-day the names of the men who constituted that great side live in the memories of those privileged to see them.

They played the game whole-heartedly, seemed to enjoy every game in which they participated, and brought to the Club an enthusiasm which has never been equalled by any of our subsequent teams.

Celtic's team of 1891-92 was a very fine one, but they did not individually or collectively compare with the record League Team.

Young, Loney and Hay will go down to history as one of the most perfect half-back lines of all time, both for vigour and science, whilst the Bennett, McMenemy, Quinn, Somers and Hamilton front line was a treat to watch in their sinuous movements and deadly attacks.

The break up of this lot came in 1912 when some of them fell back in the race. Hay went to Newcastle, Adams retired, Quinn's leg became suspect, Somers retired to Hamilton, where he later joined Accies Board, and so the great team had lost its place and we had only started to rebuild about the time the War came on, which altered the face of the game entirely.

During the War period, when the game was played under very great handicaps, Celtic were fortunate enough to have the occasional services of several famous English players occupied in war work which enabled them to play football up north occasionally, and so the Glasgow public saw Elliot of Middlesborough, Danny Shea of West Ham, Tom Barber of the Villa, David Taylor of Burnley, David McLean of Sheffield, W. Cringan and Holley of Sunderland, and one or two others from the south in the famous green and white. Scott Duncan of Dumbarton, Rangers and Third Lanark also helped us along at a time when the Government of the country felt that for the good of the folks at home and in munition works the football game should be kept going.

In the War years Celtic aided in many games for charity, and in especial for the Belgian Refugees Funds, where much money was taken in for the good cause.

Celtic as League Champions played twice against the Rest of Scotland and an Eastern Select, and also against a side representative of English teams with great success.

With the end of the War and football resuming its normal ways, Celtic again started building, and in the first year after the War again won the League Flag, which they had for the four war years, during which of course the Scottish Cup was not played for.

Rangers, who had a lot of leeway to make up with Celtic in the matter of trophy winning, made a great recovery in the race between 1919 and 1935, when they brought themselves right in line with their greatest rivals by winning both League and Scottish Cup in a fashion quite reminiscent of their Parkhead rivals, with possibly the best team the Ibrox Club have ever possessed.

Celtic, however, in this stretch of years, although they did not hit the high spots in the League race, kept popping in when the Scottish ties came round, and by victories in 1923, 1925, 1927, 1931, 1933 and 1937 kept the record for Scottish Cup victories well in hand.

Rangers also equalled another treasured Celtic record by winning the Glasgow Charity Cup for seven successive years, to equal Celtic's old record of 1911–18. Celtic, however, put themselves again on the map for this splendid trophy by winning in 1936, 1937 and 1938.

In the years since the War Celtic's biggest disappointment was the break up of their 1931 team, which looked like being the team of the future and fit to break the monopoly which Rangers were then building for themselves in Scottish football.

After a fine trip to America and Canada Celtic returned in good form and faced Rangers on 5th September at Ibrox in a League game which will be long remembered in Glasgow especially. John Thomson, the greatest of all goalkeepers playing for Celtic, in a collision with a Rangers' player near the Celtic goal sustained a head injury from which he died. Thereafter Peter Scarff, a most promising forward of sturdy build and as brave as the proverbial lion, developed tuberculosis and died in December, 1933, at the age of twenty-four, after a long and painful illness.

These occurrences almost broke Celtic for a time, but with one of their famous Cup rallies they took the Scottish Cup in 1933.

Again the team-building was taken up and at once Celtic became a power again in Scottish football, as they gained the League Flag in 1935/6 and again in 1937/8, with the Scottish Cup in 1936/7 bringing them down to 1938, their Jubilee year—when they registered their nineteenth championship of the League.

The autumn of 1938 saw them win the Glasgow Cup, which had eluded their grasp since 1931.

Their great victory in the Exhibition Empire Tourney is told in a separate page, but they have never won any trophy (except their first Scottish Cup) which has brought greater joy to their faithful and world-wide followers than this Exhibition triumph against the best of Scotland and England. They won it by a display of real Celtic spirit, and triumphed over Everton by a wonderful exhibition of the real Scottish game.

In the story of the Celtic much has been made of the famous strike of Meechan, Battles and Divers on 28th November, 1896.

This strike was caused by the vicious criticisms of an anti-Celtic writer in a Glasgow newspaper, to which the three players named took exception, but in a rather foolish way.

Just prior to the match with the Hibernians they told me they would not play unless the individual who wrote the offensive article was expelled from the Press Box. This, of course, I at once reported to the Committee, who properly refused to obey the demand, but promised that they would at their first meeting take up the matter and if necessary approach the editor of the paper in which the paragraphs appeared. The players were adamant and refused to play unless they had their way. This, of course, was an impossible position, and we at once proceeded to fill up the side as best we could. I had retired from the game but was still very fit and agreed to play, whilst Barney Crossan, another old-timer, also put on the jersey for the occasion. We had to send to Hampden for T. Dunbar, who was playing there · for the 2nd XI, and rushed him to Celtic Park for the second half of the game, which we drew.

The three culprits failed to justify their action and were dealt with, their wages being reduced to 2s. 6d. per week on legal advice.

Strange to say that was not the first strike in the Celtic, although my tale will be news to nearly all my readers now.

In 1890, when the Club was paid amateur, with Doyle and one or two others being brought back from England, the team then went on strike for equality of wages. It is farcical of course to read of an amateur team striking for wages increase, but as all the clubs with the exception of Queen's Park in those days paid their men secretly, it can be quite understood. The strike did not last long, as the Committee had to face the increases brought about by the return of Doyle & Coy.

It is not my desire in this story of the Celtic in any way to raise the position of the Club as against its greatest rivals, the Rangers, but I feel sure the readers of the history will look for some expression regarding this, the greatest of all rivalries in the game.

The two clubs have on occasion had many differences, but in the main these were only side issues which soon rectified themselves, and both sides have realized that the stern opposition was a very paying proposition.

Celtic in the early days held the lead for a number of years, but Rangers gradually crept up, but not until

1929 did they manage to get on level terms in the honours list with their Celtic friends and foes.

In the early days of the clubs' meetings their respective followers were the best of friends, and used to forgather together after the games in friendly spirit, and often-times the Brake Clubs would drive home from Hampden and other grounds after some big game between the two clubs in that sporting spirit which I have so often admired at an English Final, where victor and vanquished arm in arm spend the night after the game with each other.

In 1912 the rift in the lute appeared, and the Brake Clubs became in the main the happy hunting-ground for that breed termed " gangster " which has become such a disgrace to our city, and religion became the common battlefield for those supposed "sports". Scenes which disgraced the sport, the town and the individuals became common and the game's good name was soon tarnished.

In the last two years these things have improved a little, but a meeting of the two great rivals still brings out that vile and abominable atmosphere which has driven many decent people from the game.

I have no desire to apportion the fault, but merely ask that these people should take thought for the sake of the clubs they are supposed to support, for the sake of the game itself, and for the sake of the great city of which we are so proud. Cut it out, boys, and live and let live. Keep your muscles and sinews for the greater fight which may be with us all sooner than we expect.

Celtic were the first Scottish club to tour the Continent of Europe, playing in Vienna in 1904, where they got a wonderful reception. Later on they played in Prague,

Budapest, Berlin, Dresden, Leipzig, Hamburg, Copenhagen, Lille, Roubaix, Paris, Basle, and at Cologne, where in the last-named town they played the Select Team of the British Army of the Rhine, then stationed in that famous old cathedral town, to hold the balance between Germany and France just after the War, when this district was occupied by the Allied troops.

Celtic have also visited America and Canada, where in 1931 they made a tour of New York, Baltimore, Chicago, Brooklyn, Boston, Falls River, Detroit, Pawtucket, Toronto and Montreal.

This tour had been the dream of the early Celtic pioneers, and those privileged to travel on this occasion can never forget the hearty welcome received from their exiled friends from Scotland and Ireland. It was a real breath of home to those folks over the water and an event that will be a life-long memory to all concerned.

It will be unbelievable to those who have followed the Club to know that in our first visit to Vienna we played two games for a guarantee of £150, and it is to the credit of the men who represented the Club then, that so far from squeezing the Club for pocket allowances they actually offered to forgo their wages to be allowed to make the trip.

In 1907 we travelled to Copenhagen for a guarantee of £150. The three games played there must have drawn £3000 for our hosts.

The largest guarantee we ever got on the Continent was £1200 for three games in Prague in 1923.

Austrian football still admits a great debt to the Celtic Club for the tuition that it received from their old player

Madden, who went out there in 1905 and has stayed in Prague ever since and has helped to put the soccer game there right on the highlights of the game on the Continent.

Our only complaint against Continental football is that in 1914 we played a charity game in Budapest against Burnley, who had that year won the English Cup whilst we had won the Scottish Cup. The local club, the Ferencvarosi Torna Club, put up a beautiful cup for this, which, before a great crowd, ended in a draw. Celtic had to return home next day although Burnley had another week to play out their list of engagements. It was decided that the cup should be sent home and played for on one of the club grounds. Burnley won the toss and Celtic defeated them in September, 1914, at Burnley by 2 to nil. A proportion of the gate per agreement was sent out to the Budapest Club, but the cup never arrived. Celtic have made several applications for the trophy, and it was eventually discovered that when the War started it was put up for a charity competition to raise Red Cross funds, so that Celtic can console themselves that their trophy went in a good cause—in fact the one their Club was originated for.

The Club's early charter has never been forgotten over its fifty years, and annually a goodly sum is handed out at Christmas to the Catholic charities of the West of Scotland.

In addition to this, over the stretch of years the beneficence of the Board has been most marked, £25,000 having gone to the sacred cause from Celtic Park.

In years of disasters and public suffering many big donations have been sent out from Celtic, one of which comes to my mind in the Unemployment Rent Relief Fund in 1921, when Celtic sent £500 to the Lord Provost's fund.

The Miners' Strike also received a similar donation, whilst during the War the work of the Club for the Belgian Refugees Funds makes a tale of pride for all who follow the Celts.

Since the inception of the Celtic I claim there is no club in Scotland, or in Britain for that matter, which has done so much propaganda work as the Celts. From John o' Groats in the north right down to Stranraer at the other end of the country teams have been sent for many years to spread the light.

Some years ago, when they had a strong call from the north to tour up there in the only possible time they could, viz. in the close season, they applied to the S.F.A. for permission to do so, but were told they could only do so for public charities. This at a time when the S.F.A. were touring the Continent playing International games.

Ireland, too, has been toured from the north to the south, and many charity games have been played in Belfast between the two Celtic teams representing Glasgow and Belfast.

It is a strange thing how few Irish players have come from the Green Isle to Celtic, although when we reckon there is a Celtic team in Belfast the reason is clear.

I read in a paper lately a paragraph giving the supposed prices we had received for a big list of juniors who had left us to go South, where the insinuation was that we bred them to sell them. I defy anyone to prove that any player who ever left us did so without appreciation for the tuition he had received from us, and for the consideration he had received whilst with us and when he left us, and that he did so of his own free will and because he felt he was bettering himself.

We parted with several men who left their country for their country's good, and these of course don't come into the argument.

I have only known one Celtic player who failed to retain his love for the Club which had made him, and was not always glad to hear of its success and to come back to the old spot and renew his acquaintance with players and officials.

> We take him from the city and the plough,
> And we drill him and we dress him up so neat,
> We teach him how to use his manly brow
> And how to run and how to use his feet.

We have always been a cosmopolitan Club since our second year, and we have included in our list of players a Swede, a Jew, and a Mohammedan.

Much has been made in certain quarters about our religion, but for forty-eight years we have played a mixed team, and some of the greatest Celts we have had did not agree with us in our religious beliefs, although we have never at any time hidden what these are. Men of the type of McNair, Hay, Lyon, Buchan, Cringan, the Thomsons, or Paterson soon found out that that broadmindedness which is the real stamp of the good Christian existed to its fullest at Celtic Park, where a man was judged by his football alone.

In these days of big transfer fees it is amusing to look back and see such transfers as follow of men equally great with those for whom much greater figures are now given:

Templeton	..	.. ..	£250
Cringan	..	.. ..	£600
Shaw ..	..	.. ..	£500
P. Somers	..	.. ..	£120
J. Hay	..	.. ..	£100
J. Young	..	.. ..	£50
J. Bell	..	.. ..	£250
D. Storrier	..	.. ..	£400
J. Hodge	..	.. ..	£50
Brown, Falkirk		.. ..	£500

Celtic's fortune in the various trophies played for in the Glasgow Exhibitions of 1888 and 1901 were not of the happiest, and much ill-feeling was generated by their treatment both on and off the field by those in control.

In the 1888 contest they were slighted to such an extent by the management that they refused to play. They were at that time the prime attraction of football in Scotland, and eventually an arrangement was made to their satisfaction and they competed. In the final they got a very raw deal and lost to a team of Cowlairs specially recruited for the occasion from " a' the airts ".

In 1901 Rangers defeated them in the final where again the handling of the game caused great annoyance in Celtic ranks.

The trophy then won by the Rangers, however, eventually came into our possession, as in 1902 Rangers, to raise funds for the famous Ibrox disaster, put up the trophy for a competition between Sunderland, Everton,

Rangers and Celtic in which Celtic defeated Sunderland, and Rangers Everton to fight out the final in which Celtic won, and to-day hold this beautiful trophy amongst their most cherished possessions.

In my story I have recorded the great debt the Club owes to Mr. John Glass and Brother Walfrid, and words cannot really say all that I feel in this matter.

They were the Club's very existence for the first three years, and for some years afterwards were the binding force when the success of the Club had a tendency to bring in, by the changeable vote of the one-man-one-vote membership, many people who would only have been hindrances instead of aids to the advancement of the Club to the heights to which it has risen.

Mr. J. H. McLaughlin became the Chairman when the Club became a Limited Company, but he never held power such as did John Glass, and never was the aid to the Club the cheery East End joiner was all his days.

Mr. McLaughlin did much good work, however, in the S.F.A. and League, where his strong silent manner made him a very useful member when much thinking was to be done.

He was very badly treated by the S.F.A. members. When on an occasion he was nominated for the Treasurership he was badly let down through a clique, who canvassed very strongly against him secretly and beat him at the vote decisively.

I also suffered the fate of other Celtic representatives when I was by a clique of country clubs outvoted for a seat on the League Management Committee on which I had sat with great success and with the admiration and goodwill of the English as well as Scottish clubs, after 14 years' service.

This, however, was not the only time a Celtic representative worthy of official honours was let down, as two years ago Mr. John Shaughnessy, reckoned a safe candidate for Vice-Presidential honours, was also given the order of the knock by underhand canvassing.

I also enjoyed long service in the Scottish League and had the honour of being the first player to sit in the Chair of the League body and International League Committee, which I did from 1921 to 1924, when I retired.

The years that have elapsed since the Club's formation into a Limited Liability Company have seen great changes in the personnel of the Board of Management.

The passing of the old brigade in the persons of John Glass, John O'Hara, J. H. McLaughlin, Jas. Kelly, T. E. Maley, John McKillop, James Grant and M. Dunbar left sad gaps in their ranks, but the coming of Mr. Tom White and Mr. Tom Colgan brought to the management a virile and more youthful outlook which has brought much success to the Club.

Much could be written of the doings of the Club under those great enthusiasts who have gone, but the best that may be said of them is they have left behind them in Celtic Park of to-day a lasting monument to work well done, to love of the Club they almost worshipped, and to their names, which will ever be enshrined in the story of this Club, the equal of anything in broad Scotland in every shape and form, and which has gained its present proud position by sheer effort and against much unworthy opposition.

The only point which one might criticize in those who are gone is the lack of vision to see the possibilities of the game developing as it has done, otherwise Celtic might have been to-day the leaders, as they were the pioneers, in the scheme of greater grounds for the housing of the Internationals and great finals.

" Sufficient for the day ", however, fits the tale, and Celtic can with pride point to the fact that their pioneer work has gained for Scotland such grounds as Hampden and Ibrox, which are a credit to the game and the best in the world to-day.

Celtic's first big cup win was in the Glasgow Cup on 14th February, 1891, when at Hampden Park they won this cup, defeating Third Lanark by 4–0.

In Celtic's first year they played the following Scottish Cup ties:

Cowlairs, Celtic Park, 22nd Sept., 1888. Won 8–0.
Clyde, Celtic Park, 4th Nov. Lost 0–1.
    Protested on state of ground and replayed 8th Decr., 1888, winning by 9–2.
East Stirlingshire. Away, 15th Decr., 1888. Won 2–1.
Dumbarton, 12th Jany., 1889. Away. Won 4–1.
Final at Hampden Park with Third Lanark, 2nd Feby. Snow Final. Lost 0–3. 9th Feby., re-played. Lost 1–2.

Celtic's First Scottish Cup win, 1891–92.

Queens Park, 12th March, 1892. Won 1–0 at Ibrox Park.
Protested. Replayed and won by 5–1, 9th April, 1892.

Celtic's First Glasgow Charity Cup win, 1st June, 1892.
Defeated Rangers at Hampden Park by 2–0.

Celtic's First League Championship, 1892–3.
Won with 29 points.

Celtic's record score in Scottish League.
Against Dundee, 26th Octr., 1895.   11–0.

The coming of the Celtic as a first-class club was of course made comparatively easy by the state of Scottish football in 1888. There was no restriction in those days to taking a player away from another club, as at that time all players were, or were supposed to be, amateurs.

This state of things existed up to 1890, when the Scottish League was formed. Thereafter a player had to be bought from the League club that held his signature, and, as to-day, even at the end of the season his club could hold him by making a certain offer or placing him on the transfer list at a fee.

Just prior to the formation of the Scottish League in 1890, Celtic managed to persuade Dan Doyle, Alec Brady, John Madden and Neil McCallum to return from England to their native heath, and from that foundation the great Celtic team of 1892 was built.

This team was the first to win the three cups in one season and just missed adding the League Flag, an unlucky defeat at Leith putting us out of the final bid.

With the formation of the Club into a Limited Company the Board went on bolder lines, and players were brought from the South who helped to make further history for our Club; of these men the names of Welford,

Orr, Goldie, Allan, Bell, Storrier, Fisher, Reynolds, will revive memories to those of the old brigade.

We also brought Ching Morrison from Belfast Glentoran, the first native Irishman to wear the Celtic colours.

The period between 1896 and 1902 found the Club relying chiefly on players brought back from England after years of service there, and getting to the end of their playing career. Most of them did well with the Celtic, but only for a very few years, when their places had to be filled.

I always felt that what we gained at the moment in the services of these seasoned players was lost to us by the fact that their possible time of service with us was very limited, and during it we had no chance of raising lads to fill their places. This it was that induced me to try and get our Board to go out for the young ones, and by recruiting these right from their junior club ensure for our team youth with all its vigour and the *esprit de corps* which has always been to me one of the greatest assets in our players.

Men like Dave Russell, Harry Marshall, Jim Welford, Hugh Goldie, John Bell, Davie Storrier, the two Kings, Jack Reynolds, were for a period good servants of the Club, but when they lost their form they were absolutely finished and then we had to replace almost the whole team.

From 1902 this policy has been maintained and the results speak for themselves. We have raised many teams from the " raw ", and what they could not give in scientific play they made up for by their enthusiasm and the will to win. Some of the young ones taken on shaped badly at first but they learned their lessons and came on all right in time. One of the best examples is James McStay, who came to us as a wing half. He did very badly for some time and after a game at Kirkcaldy the Board decided he was not able " to make the grade ". I pleaded for a further trial and as events have proved he did make good and came to be one of our most valuable men.

Another point against the engagement of players who had previous long service was that when they left us their value in League rights was nil; whereas there are very few juniors of any standing but a Club like ours can recover some of the cash spent on them.

Many very interesting stories could be told regarding Celtic players in the days when poaching in Scotland and in England was quite common. This was in the days before the inception of the League in Scotland in 1890. The English League was formed in 1888, and for the next two years Scottish clubs waged a sort of re-taliatory war on their Saxon friends who were constantly taking Scottish players to England, where they had professionalism five years before the slower-moving Scottish Association woke up to the necessity of being honest in this matter.

Sandy McMahon was poached away by Notts Forest, who had previously taken away Neilly McCallum. Celtic could stand for McCallum's defection, but McMahon, then at his best, was a " soo o' anither sort ".

Promptly messengers were secretly sent South, and after much trouble discovered that McMahon was being kept in the country in order to hold him safely until he

committed himself for Notts Forest in a game on Saturday. The scouts discovered his lair but then found he
had been taken into Nottingham for the day. They
followed there only to see him going back by a train
on the opposite side of the arrival platform: once again
to the country, they this time " woo'ed " the " Duke "
(as he was known by the football fans of his day) back to
Scotland to play many wonderful games for the Celtic.

Jerry Reynolds was " lifted " from Carfin on a Friday
night, before a Glasgow Cup tie with Queen's Park, from
his collier row there. He was called to the door by John
Glass after midnight and coaxed, in his shirt and trousers,
to join Celtic at once, and he agreed and drove off safely
with his captors, who would have had a rough time if
the Carfinites had caught them.

Before Neil McCallum was taken to Nottingham a
Notts agent had foolishly arranged to meet him at Celtic
Park after the game and to make an offer of terms. His
letter was handed by Neilly's landlord to John Glass,
and the agent was captured and narrowly missed being
tarred and feathered, so strong was the feeling in those
days.

Rangers and Celtic had a great duel over the signing
of the late Bobby Neil, a great centre-half who had
played for Hibs and then gone to Liverpool, from where
he was being coaxed home on a free transfer by the two
great rivals.

He was to meet both clubs in Steel's Hotel, Argyle
Street, on 1st May, the first date he could be signed on
by the Scottish clubs.

Their representatives were there, and much haggling

took place in which Celtic seemed to be the highest
bidders, but just when Celtic thought they had him a
fresh bid from Rangers caught the " big fish ", and Neil
fixed for the team in which he played a great part in the
half-back division of Rangers, Gibson, Neil and Robertson, which I think has never been equalled in any of
their teams since.

Jacky Robertson was another source of contention
between Celtic and Rangers when he was anxious to
finish with Everton.   Again Celtic seemed to have the
" inside course " so dear to a jockey, but again fates
decided otherwise and Jacky signed for Ibrox, who
thereby secured a world beater.

Celtic lost another great player in Sandy Turnbull of
Hurlford by the proverbial hairbreadth.   I went down
to Hurlford to sign this great player, and got him just
home from the pits he wrought in and he seemed willing
to sign on.   Whilst cleaning up, however, Tom Hynds,
an old Celtic player, whom my brother Tom had taken
when he went to manage Manchester City, arrived on
the scene.   A wire from Hurlford to Manchester had
brought him down in haste, and the local influence took
Turnbull to Manchester, where he proved one of the
best catches England had secured from the North.

Dan Doyle came back to Celtic in 1890 from Everton,
in which team with Andrew Hannah he had won an
English League medal in 1889.   Dan wearied for home,
but he was in great request in England.   He had actually
fixed to go to Bolton Wanderers, the first team he had
played with in England, but home ties decided him and
he came back to Scotland to play as an *amateur for Celtic*.

I don't think Everton had a man in those days as popular as the Airdrie lad, and there were loud lamentations when he " lifted his graith " and returned to Scotland.

In the early League days players could bargain for a fixed transfer which enabled them to shift at the end of a season for a fixed sum, provided they did not get suitable terms. It was in this way that Bennett left Celtic to go to Ibrox, and it was in this way that George Livingstone managed to play for Hearts, Sunderland, Celtic, Liverpool and Rangers.

Charley Shaw came to Celtic on a fixed transfer of £500 from Queen's Park Rangers and proved a very cheap investment, and his work in combination with McNair and Dodds will always be remembered by Celtic followers as the greatest of its kind.

Celtic fixed John Brown of Falkirk on the same lines for £500, but rued their bargain and sold him two years afterwards for £1600 to Chelsea—another good bargain.

Celtic's cheapest player ever was their greatest centre forward, James Quinn, who signed the League form for Celtic for £2, doing so, however, on the statement which he made (to get rid of me) that he would never play senior. I held back the form until I later persuaded the " one and only " to become definitely a Celt.

Peter Somers was lent to Blackburn Rovers at the end of a season to help them out and signed for them for next season. When he wanted to return to Celtic, Rovers let him go at the cheap price of £120. What a catch for Celtic, as he did much to make up the famous Bennett, McMenemy, Quinn, Somers and Hamilton line.

Willie Cringan was Celtic's most expensive player as

they paid Sunderland £600 for him after the War, during which Cringan had played for a year or so for Celtic as an army man.

Celtic paid their amateur players in their first years firstly 30s. per week and latterly after a " strike " £3 per week.

For the winning of the Scottish Cup in 1892 the Celtic team each got a bonus of £3 and a new suit of clothes.

John Madden of Dumbarton agreed to play for Celtic in the 1888 Exhibition Tourney and met the party on arrival at the Exhibition. He was called away by a friend and did not turn up for dressing at the pavilion. He had been kidnapped by Dumbarton. Celtic had their revenge when Celtic in that season beat Dumbarton 4 to 1 in the Scottish Cup at Dumbarton with Madden playing against them.

Celtic and Aberdeen have always been very good friends, and one action of the Celtic possibly made this doubly strong when years ago, before a cup tie which they had to play against the Dons, there was handed to them a certain protest against one of the Aberdeen players, Jock Hume.

Celtic wrote previous to the tie and gave Aberdeen the information given them, and stated they would not protest against this player and Aberdeen could play him if they wished. They did and Celtic won the tie and Aberdeen's gratitude and admiration.

Quite a different spirit from that of a club in the early days who on the day of a Scottish Cup tie protested along with Celtic on the condition of the ground. The referee played the game and Celtic were beaten, to find after the game that their opponents had got back from the referee their early protest. However, the S.F.A. would have none of this, and the tie was replayed and Celtic won through.

Celtic had still another protested tie which ended sensationally. In the Scottish ties they met Clyde at Celtic Park (old), where on a regular quagmire Clyde won by 1–0 chiefly through a wonderful display by goalkeeper Chalmers, who latterly went to Rangers. On a protest the referee admitted he could not see lines, &c., and only finished the game as he was afraid of the spectators. The replay saw Celtic win by 9–2 and yet in the replay Chalmers played a great game.

The start of the break up completely of the Great Team came with Quinn's retirement and later on with Sunny Jim's tragic accident at Paisley which forced his retirement too. One can be spared dwelling on the story of these two men who had done so much for the Club they loved.

Sunny Jim was picked up at Bristol, where he had gone for a short trial with one of the Bristol clubs, but got homesick and wanted home. Celtic were down there trying to get Bob Muir, an old Killie outside right, to return home, and when he agreed to do so Sunny, who was standing by, happened to remark he wished he was going too. They brought him back and gained for the Club the most enthusiastic clubman they ever had. Jamie would play night or day, in sunshine or rain, and never spared himself. He was a source of inspiration to the rest of the team and never ceased to urge them on to greater effort. He was a man and a half in any team, and his place has never been filled since the fatal day he twisted his knee at Paisley and had to give up the game to die tragically through a motor-cycle accident a few years later at Hurlford.

To tell the story of James Quinn would take almost a book itself, but to put it as shortly as possible we might say that Celtic lost half a team when James Quinn retired full of honours and with the never-dying love of every good sport who ever saw him play.

The picture of Quinn set for goal with his sturdy, well-knit frame in the perfect condition he always kept himself in, and striving all the way to keep the ball in control as he charged off the attacking defenders, was a sight never to be forgotten, and when to crown all the finishing effort of a cannon-ball shot came from him he would be a very cold-blooded enthusiast who could refrain from cheering the sturdy collier laddie whom I signed for £2 a week in the row where he was reared.

As I have often said, all the men Jamie Quinn killed lived a long time, and although he was credited with doing all sorts of things to opponents I have never heard any of them giving him a bad name. He took and gave and in only one case did I see him transgress the rules, and even the man he charged very vigorously afterwards admitted he only got what he deserved.

TOM E. MALEY

One of the pioneers of the Club. Acted on Committee and also as
Treasurer. Played 3 years for Club. Was first Celtic official to sit on
Scottish and Glasgow Associations

JOHN O'HARA

Served on Committee from 1888
until 1897, and as Director from
1897 until death in 1904

ARTHUR MURPHY

Committee from 1890 until 1897

J. H. McLAUGHLIN

Acted on Committee as Treasurer for 3 years and as Chairman
from 1897 until his death in 1909

JOHN McKILLOP
Director from 1897 until death in 1914

Office-bearers

OFFICE-BEARERS IN 1890–91

Hon. Patrons.

His Grace the Archbishop of Glasgow.

Michael Davitt, Esq.

Hon. President.

Dr. John Conway.

President.

John Glass.

Vice-President.

James Quillan.

Treasurer.

Hugh Darroch.

Secretary.

John O'Hara.

Match Secretary.

William Maley.

Committee.

J. M. Nelis.	J. Shaughnessy.
M. Cairns.	J. H. M'Laughlin.
W. M'Killop.	T. E. Maley.
Daniel Malloy.	John M'Donald.
Joseph M'Grory.	David Meikleham.
P. Welsh.	

47

OFFICE-BEARERS IN 1891–92

Patrons.

His Grace the Archbishop of Glasgow.

Michael Davitt, Esq.

Hon. President.

Joseph Shaughnessy.

President.

John Glass.

Vice-President.

T. E. Maley.

Hon. Secy.

J. H. M'Laughlin.

Match Secy.

William Maley.

Treasurer.

James M'Kay.

Committee.

S. J. Henry.	Tim Walls.
A. Murphy.	John M'Quade.
James Kelly.	James Moore.
John O'Hara.	James Cairns.

As Leaseholders.

J. M. Nelis.	W. M'Killop.
D. Meikleham.	G. Bradley.

OFFICE-BEARERS IN 1892–93

Hon. Patron.

HIS GRACE THE ARCHBISHOP OF GLASGOW.

Hon. President.

JOSEPH SHAUGHNESSY.

President.

JOHN GLASS.

Vice-President.

T. E. MALEY.

Hon. Secretary.

J. H. M'LAUGHLIN.

Hon. Treasurer.

JAMES M'KAY.

Match Secretary.

WILLIAM MALEY.

Committee.

S. J. HENRY.	ARTHUR MURPHY.
JAMES KELLY.	JOHN O'HARA.
T. WALLS.	J. M'QUADE.
J. CAIRNS.	J. CURTIS.
J. M. NELIS.	W. M'KILLOP.
D. MEIKLEHAM.	G. BRADLEY.

(The last four as Leaseholders.)

OFFICE-BEARERS IN 1893–94

Patrons.

His Grace the Archbishop of Glasgow.

Michael Davitt, Esq.

Hon. President.

Wm. M'Killop.

President.

John Glass.

Vice-President.

J. H. M'Laughlin.

Hon. Secy.

William Maley.

Hon. Treasurer.

James M'Kay.

Committee.

A. Murphy.	J. M'Quade.
S. J. Henry.	James Cairns.
T. E. Maley.	James Moore.
J. Kelly.	P. Gallacher.
J. O'Hara.	Tim Walls.

Leaseholders.

J. M. Nelis.	G. Bradley.
D. Meikleham.	J. Shaughnessy.

OFFICE-BEARERS IN 1894–95

Patrons.

His Grace the Archbishop of Glasgow.

Michael Davitt, Esq.

Hon. President.

Wm. M'Killop.

President.

John Glass.

Vice-President.

J. H. M'Laughlin.

Hon. Secretary.

William Maley.

Hon. Treasurer.

James M'Kay.

Committee.

A. Murphy.	J. O'Hara.
M. Dunbar.	J. Curtis.
J. M'Cann.	P. Gallacher.
J. Kelly.	T. Walls.
F. M'Erlean.	J. Moore.

Leaseholders.

J. M. Nelis.	G. Bradley.
D. Meikleham.	J. Shaughnessy.

OFFICE-BEARERS IN 1895–96

Patrons.

His Grace the Archbishop of Glasgow.

Michael Davitt, Esq.

Hon. President.

Wm. M'Killop.

President.

John Glass.

Vice-President.

J. H. M'Laughlin.

Hon. Secy.

William Maley.

Hon. Treasurer.

James M'Kay.

Committee.

M. Dunbar.	P. Gallacher.
J. M'Cann.	F. M'Erlean.
A. Murphy.	J. M'Grory.
John M'Creadie.	G. Doherty.
John M'Quade.	John M'Bride.
J. Curtis.	

OFFICE-BEARERS IN 1896–97

Patrons.

HIS GRACE THE ARCHBISHOP OF GLASGOW.

MICHAEL DAVITT, ESQ.

Hon. President.

WM. M'KILLOP.

President.

JOHN GLASS.

Vice-President.

J. H. M'LAUGHLIN.

Hon. Secretary.

WILLIAM MALEY.

Hon. Treasurer.

JAMES M'KAY.

Committee.

M. DUNBAR.	P. GALLACHER.
J. GRANT.	F. M'ERLEAN.
A. MURPHY.	P. M'MORROW.
JOHN M'CREADIE.	F. HAVELIN.
JOHN M'QUADE.	J. WARNOCK.
J. CURTIS.	

PROVISIONAL BOARD, 1897

J. H. M'LAUGHLIN.	JOHN GLASS.
JOHN O'HARA.	MICHAEL DUNBAR.
T. E. MALEY.	JAMES M'KAY.
MICHAEL HUGHES.	

CHAIRMEN SINCE THE INCEPTION OF CLUB, 1888

DR. CONWAY.	1888 and 1889.
JOHN GLASS.	1890 to 1897.
J. H. M'LAUGHLIN.	1897 to 1909.
JAMES KELLY.	1909 to 1914.
THOMAS WHITE.	1914 to date.

MATCH SECRETARY, HON. SECRETARY AND SECRETARY-MANAGER, 1888 TO DATE

WILLIAM MALEY.

FIRST BOARD OF DIRECTORS

JOHN O'HARA.	Died 1904.
JOHN GLASS.	Died 1906.
J. H. M'LAUGHLIN.	Died 1909.
JAMES GRANT.	Died 1914.
JOHN M'KILLOP.	Died 1914.
MICHAEL DUNBAR.	Died 1921.
JAMES KELLY.	Died 1931.

LIST OF DIRECTORS SINCE FORMATION OF LIMITED COMPANY

JOHN O'HARA.	1897 to 1904.
JOHN GLASS.	1897 to 1906.
J. H. M'LAUGHLIN.	1897 to 1909.
JAMES GRANT.	1897 to 1914.
JOHN M'KILLOP.	1897 to 1914.
MICHAEL DUNBAR.	1897 to 1921.
JAMES KELLY.	1897 to 1931.
TOM E. MALEY.	1897 (Provisional).
MICHAEL HUGHES.	1897 (Provisional).
JAMES M'KAY.	1897 (Provisional).
THOMAS COLGAN.	1904 to date.
THOMAS WHITE.	1906 to date.
JOHN SHAUGHNESSY.	1911 to date.
JOHN M'KILLOP.	1921 to date.
ROBERT KELLY.	1931 to date.

TRAINERS

The following were trainers of the team from 1888 to date:

JOSEPH ANDERSON.	D. FREIL.
T. MAGUIRE.	R. DAVIS.
J. J. MULLEN.	W. QUINN.
E. M'GARVIE.	P. FARMER.
J. QUASKLEY.	J. M'MENEMY.

Celtic Honours, 1888-1938

Scottish Cup
15 times, record

1892	1899	1900	1904	1907
1908	1911	1912	1914	1923
1925	1927	1931	1933	1937

Scottish League Championship
19 times

1892–93	1893–94	1895–96	1897–98	1904–5
1905–6	1906–7	1907–8	1908–9	1909–10
1913–14	1914–15	1915–16	1916–17	1918–19
1921–22	1925–26	1935–36	1937–38	

Glasgow Cup
18 times

1890	1891	1894	1895	1904
1905	1906	1907	1909	1915
1916	1919	1920	1926	1927
	1928	1930	1938	

Glasgow Charity Cup
23 times, record

1892	1893	1894	1895	1896
1899	1903	1905	1908	1912
1913	1914	1915	1916	1917
1918	1920	1921	1924	1926
	1936	1937	1938	

Our League History

THE institution of the Scottish Football League can be likened to the foundation of the Celtic Club in that they both marked the beginning of a new era in football, the former being responsible for a more orderly arrangement of fixtures, and the latter introducing an enterprise in the building up of teams hitherto unknown to any great extent.

Moreover, it would not be too much to say that the entry of the Celtic Club into the arena added a zest to football in Scotland which resulted in an anxiety to follow the example of the English clubs who had two years earlier taken the step which was to lead to the development of a scheme later to embrace the whole country.

The sensational results gained by the Club in its first season and the series of misfortunes experienced in the next, while merely whetting the appetite of its promoters, filled its competitors with an almost unbelievable antipathy not unmixed with envy, with the result that although Celtic were included, for very obvious reasons, in the original ten clubs which formed the League, it may well be imagined how intense was the desire to defeat them on every occasion.

The team which had gradually altered from the original band of heroes made an unexpectedly indifferent start, and further handicapped by a penalty imposed for playing an ineligible player, finished behind Rangers and Dumbarton, who shared the first championship.

Season 1891–92 again started disastrously, but the recruits of the previous year, Sandy McMahon and Johnny Campbell, had now developed into a great left wing. McCallum had returned and with Alec Brady made up a right wing with which Madden as leader formed an attack second to none in the country.

Dan Doyle, brought from Everton with Brady, was supreme with Jerry Reynolds in defence, and Joe Cullen was the new goalkeeper. The first half of the League programme following the early reverse was a succession of victories, but after the Scottish Cup twice-played final, which was to give us our first major honour, the team fell away, and were pipped on the post for the Flag by Dumbarton.

Success was to follow in the next season, 1892–93. It was a happy augury for the future, as it marked the opening of the new ground, and with the legalization of professionalism, influenced by convincing arguments of J. H. McLaughlin, football seemed in a fair way to becoming a more honest and better organized sport.

Joe Cassidy, Jimmy Blessington and Johnny Divers had joined the Club, and in the following season Dan McArthur became a Celt along with Peter O'Rourke Charley McElevy and Willie Ferguson.

The Club's second League Championship followed in the next season, 1893–94, Hearts being runners up with St. Bernards and Rangers well behind.

Jerry Reynolds left for Burnley at the end of this

season and Johnny Campbell joined Aston Villa. Of the original team only James Kelly remained in active service, but there was no lack of recruits, as Peter Meechan, Barney Battles, " Ching " Morrison and John King were added to the staff.

We were only able, despite this intensive recruiting, to finish second on the table in 1894–95, Hearts winning the Flag, and possibly our failure was due more to a superfluity of talent rather than a scarcity, as, while we had won the Flag in the previous season with 19 players, we found ourselves unable to repeat the performance with 35—three goalkeepers were required to keep us going, four backs, twelve half-backs and sixteen forwards.

Continuing to strengthen the team, Barney Battles, Allan Martin, Davie Russell, Alec King and Paddy Gilhooly joined the Club, and in 1895–96 the Championship was regained with the highest aggregate of points for a ten-club League.

Several slips during the earlier part of the season were nullified by a succession of victories which followed, including the defeat of Dundee at Parkhead by 11 goals to 0. Six points only were surrendered during the campaign.

The Club, by its success in winning the Championship thrice in six years, was now firmly established as a playing force, and it was significant that the Vice-President, Mr. J. H. McLaughlin, was chosen to succeed Mr. Alexander Lawrance as the second President of the League.

The season 1896–97 was one remarkable for the success of the Edinburgh clubs, Hearts winning the Flag with 28 points, Hibernian coming second with 26.

We finished fourth, Rangers, with 25 points, being one ahead, but there is no doubt that but for an incident unprecedented in football we would have finished on top.

I refer to the " strike " in which three of our players, Battles, Meechan and Divers, as a protest against the unfair, even brutal, criticism of a certain section of the Press, refused to turn out against Hibernian at Parkhead unless the representatives of the offending paper were ejected from the Press Box.

To this the management could not consent, although they had considerable sympathy with the malcontents, and promised to make representation in the proper quarters.

The players, however, were adamant in their decision, and after some delay, although I had given up the game, I turned out along with Barney Crossan, while a message was hurriedly dispatched to Hampden Park for Tommy Dunbar, who was playing there for our second eleven, and he arrived long after the game had started.

The result was a draw, and those of the remaining matches were not in keeping with our previous returns —the affair costing us the Championship, as the players were naturally suspended and the playing strength suffered in consequence.

This year witnessed the flotation of the Club, and under the new regime an intensive enlistment of new players was entered upon, the Directors being determined to place the Club in a position which would enable them to maintain and even improve the high reputation they had won during their short career.

George Allan was brought from Liverpool, Hugh

Goldie from Everton, Willie Orr and Adam Henderson from Preston North End.

Johnny Campbell was persuaded to return from Aston Villa, and with him came Jack Reynolds, who had the distinction of having represented both Ireland and England in International matches, and Jim Welford.

Another player who joined our ranks and who was afterwards to become famous was Peter Somers, and the season of 1897–98 was entered upon with great confidence.

This confidence was justified by the winning of the Championship with still another record in points for the number of clubs, only three being lost in the tournament.

It is interesting to note that in this season the New Year's Day match at Parkhead with Rangers attracted a record attendance of 42,000.

A most indifferent start in the early games of 1898–99 completely ruined our chances of retaining our title— indeed this was the beginning of a rather lean series of years for us so far as the League was concerned.

Strangely enough, it coincided with a remarkable run of successes by our great rivals Rangers, who carried away the Championship during the next four seasons.

It is not difficult to account for our falling off, the fact being that a number of the players who had been responsible for our previous successes had attained the age when their usefulness was impaired, and great difficulty was experienced in replacing them by youngsters of the necessary skill.

During the comparatively short life of the Club a type of game had been established, a game which even in our early days was regarded as at least the equal to that of the famous Preston North End.

But the Directors were by no means idle. They included men who knew football, and would not be satisfied until they had built up a side which was capable of producing and maintaining the standard of their great predecessors.

And so it came about that while we were unable to add to our Championship honours, a policy of rearing our own recruits was evolved and maintained, and a glorious reward was the result following this period of reconstruction.

Good players came and departed, but the work of gathering together lads of the necessary type went on, and honours referred to elsewhere came our way—but not the Championship.

By degrees, however, the men who were to make history drifted to Parkhead. Jimmy Quinn, Willie Loney, Davie Hamilton, James McMenemy arrived at the beginning of the present century to be followed by Alec Bennett, Davie Adams, Jimmy Young, Jimmy Hay, Alec McNair, Donald McLeod and others.

We had been challenging Rangers strongly, and in 1903–04 had finished level with them, although Third Lanark carried off the Flag, but in the following season the great tug-of-war was staged.

Our team which had won the Scottish Cup in the previous April averaged 22 years, and were accordingly fit for a long drawn out battle.

At the end of the League campaign Rangers and Celtic were level on points, and after a deciding game we were acclaimed champions for the first time in eight years.

It was a victory worth waiting for, and accomplished under conditions which left no doubt in the minds of the public that it was the forerunner of many more.

With a margin of twelve points from our Ibrox rivals we carried away the Flag in the following season, and during the next four completed a record that has never been equalled—that of winning the Championship on six successive occasions.

No apology is necessary for dwelling on this wonderful achievement, the magnitude of which is confirmed by the fact that it stands alone in the 48 years of the League's existence.

It is all the more notable owing to our winning margin over our greatest rivals following the first of the series, which was gained only after a deciding game. Hearts, Falkirk twice and Aberdeen respectively finishing second in the other five seasons.

Only once during that period did we fail to gain an additional honour—in 1908-09—when after a drawn battle with Rangers in the final the Cup was withheld following the regrettable Hampden riot.

I mention this in order to show that our players not only proved their consistency in the League competition but in others also, and it will ever stand as a memento to the judgment and foresight of the management that the number of players included in the teams of that wonderful six seasons was comparatively small.

The Scottish Football League marked their appreciation of the feat by presenting the Club with a shield on which the names of all the players who had taken part in the six years' campaign are recorded.

It was not to be expected that the success of the previous six years could be maintained, and with the departure of Bennett midway through the run and his successor, Willie Kivlichan, Jimmy Hay, Dan Munro and the practical retiral of Peter Somers, some time had to elapse before a team capable of standing up to the strain of a fierce League competition could be built up.

Elsewhere it is told, however, that already by winning other honours the work of the management was meeting with success, and there was a promise of another great combine which, wearing our famous colours, might even outshine its predecessor.

Towards the end of our record run Joe Dodds, Peter Johnstone, Andy M'Atee, John Brown, Tom McGregor and John Mulrooney had been discovered, and were by this time able to take their places in the team, and in November, 1911, a slip of a lad, who was afterwards to carve a niche in the history of the game, was signed, and forced his way almost immediately into the League side. I refer to " Patsy " Gallagher.

Followed Charley Shaw, John Browning, John M'Master, James M'Coll, Willie Angus, and Joe Cassidy; 1913–14 saw us start our League programme fairly well until we met with a couple of defeats by St. Mirren and Hearts over a week-end.

They did us no harm—the reverse in fact—as in our next twenty-three games only two points were conceded—by draws with Motherwell and Partick Thistle; and then disaster overtook us at Falkirk, where we lost by 1–0.

Then another unbeaten run with but two draws, and once again we claimed the title of Champions.

With all our " regulars " and a few new recruits to bring along, our prospects for 1914–15 were bright indeed, but as the season was on the point of beginning the drums of war resounded throughout the land.

A number of the lads answered the call immediately, although no one realized that it was going to last so long, and as time went on our ranks were depleted gradually.

Still the game went on—it was the expressed wish of the authorities—but those who remained at home did their bit in the factories and workshops that were so necessary for the service of the country.

The other clubs were similarly affected, so that the League competition was just as keen as before, and in 1914–15 we retained our title, Rangers finishing second six points behind.

During this campaign we used only sixteen players, among them being Jimmy Quinn, who now retired from active service after giving us his best for a period extending over fourteen years.

The season 1915–16 was even more successful from a playing point of view. Although we were often in sore straits to field a team, the players, sometimes almost complete strangers to our regulars but proud to wear our colours, with traditional enthusiasm upheld our reputation so well that another title was won, and with the loss of only eight points in 38 games.

There was a tremendous rush at the end of the season in order to complete our fixtures, so much so indeed that we were actually forced to play two League games on 15th April.

The first, against Raith Rovers at Celtic Park, we won by 6–o, and in the evening at Fir Park our representatives completed an excellent day's work by defeating Motherwell by 3–1.

Considerable difficulty was experienced in getting together a team for 1916–17, owing to continued depletion, but making use of several players working in the district— as did the other clubs—we managed to instil into them the Celtic spirit, and for the fourth successive season won the Championship.

It was not to be expected that our success in the League competition could go on indefinitely, relying as we did on so few players, and in 1917–18 we had to be content with second place, although the winners— Rangers—only beat us by a single point.

The season's competition was remarkable owing to the fact that with the Flag virtually won so early as January, a series of misfortunes ended in narrow defeat.

A certain amount of consolation was, however, derived from the fact that the League Charity Shield, which was instituted for the benefit of players' dependants who had suffered in the Great War, was won by us, a fitting honour for a Club whose inspiration—never forgotten nor neglected—was charity.

Although 1918–19 was to witness the end of the world slaughter, it was some time before we could be said to have returned to normal conditions.

The League had been reduced to 18 clubs in the previous season, but even with the curtailed programme it was still difficult for us to rely on a regular side.

Other clubs were more fortunate in this respect,

indeed some were stronger in a playing sense than for several years.

Several of our most promising and talented men had made the great sacrifice—while others, including McStay, Cringan, Dodds, M'Master, Cassidy, M'Atee, Ribchester, &c., were still wearing the uniform.

Despite these difficulties and losses we started not so badly, losing seven points up to the New Year, but after drawing with Rangers at Ibrox on 1st January, 1919, we went right ahead and finished undefeated, dropping only other two points through draws, and once again won the Championship—our fifteenth success in the competition.

It was only to be expected that following the conclusion of war a process of rebuilding would require to be faced, as those who had carried the flag during those four awful years could not fail to show the strain.

Dodds, Cringan, M'Atee, Cassidy and the others returned to Parkhead naturally, but the Directors wisely began to rebuild, and, in addition to a few youngsters picked up during the previous season, added to the list a few others who were in the very near future to bring fame to the Club.

From St. Anthony's came Tommy M'Inally, Johnny M'Kay and John Gilchrist, along with " Tully " Craig of Tullibody and Davie Pratt from Lochore, all of whom had been eagerly sought after by clubs from all parts.

Our start in the League race was not very auspicious, and by the middle of the season Rangers were hailed as Champions. The prophets failed to reckon on our staying power, however, and a wonderful run of successes by our lads gave them a severe fright—they won the Flag by only three points in the end (71–68), Aberdeen being third with 57.

The following season saw the end of James M'Menemy's playing career so far as the Celtic Club was concerned, the Directors deciding that the time had arrived when he would require to make way for younger players.

They presented him with a free transfer, and we take a certain amount of credit for the fact that by the end of the season he had assisted materially in winning the Scottish Cup for Partick Thistle.

M'Nair was therefore the last of the old brigade who assisted in making that famous record, yet unbeaten, but the work of building still went on—Archie Longmuir, " Jean " M'Farlane and Jimmy Murphy being added to the staff.

Starting well in the campaign of 1920–21, a series of draws where victories were possible and actually deserved cost many valuable points, and even after winning a brilliant victory at Ibrox on New Year's Day, the same carelessness permitted our Ibrox rivals to draw ahead after being in arrears, and go on to win the Flag—this was one of our worst years in the competition.

While there was still a fair sprinkling of older players on our list of 1921–22 it was evident that youth was going to force its way, and still another batch of youngsters came into the fold, such as Jimmy M'Stay, Hugh Hilley, Alec Thomson, John Connor, Frank Collins from Dublin, Sam Glasgow and John M'Knight.

This season marked our sixteenth Championship, and although the honour was gained by the narrowest possible margin (owing to the inconsistency displayed during the season when many points were lost through pure carelessness) it was undoubtedly deserved.

There is no doubt that a somewhat difficult period had been reached, as so many changes were forced on the Directors, and possibly the younger players had not yet realized what was necessary in a Celtic team.

Success affects people in different ways, as was experienced when M'Inally attempted to dictate terms to the Directors, an ill-advised step which was answered in the only possible way—he was transferred.

Three youngsters who were afterwards to make history were included in the list of 1922-23—James M'Grory, Willie Crilly and Paddy Connolly—but somehow a lassitude seemed to settle on the players, not at all in keeping with the spirit displayed by their predecessors.

It has to be admitted, however, that they were most unfortunate with regard to injuries round about this time, and the task of discovering the proper blend, which the Directors had set themselves, meant changed teams and did not make for harmonious play.

Whatever the reason the show made in the League from 1922 to 1925 was far from satisfactory—indeed all round honours were fewer in this period, and apparently without cause, than since almost the beginning of the Club.

The determination of the Directors to rear their own players in future, if it did not bring immediate success, was a wise one, as it enabled them to pick and choose among the junior lads who they believed would put their hearts into their work, and it must be remembered that opposed to them year by year were teams of the ready-made order.

Each year young players were engaged in order to discover the true blend. Peter Wilson, Peter Shevlin, Eddie Gilfeather were the latest newcomers, and it was not until 1925–26 that they came into their own once more.

We practically reversed the pointage of Rangers and ourselves, Hearts and Motherwell being our nearest opponents eight points behind, our Ibrox rivals counting six less than these.

Our youthful side changed the order of things in this season, fighting like veterans in the points competition, to fail in the most disappointing manner in Cup finals.

M'Inally, seeing the error of his ways, had returned to the fold, but one of our greatest players, Patsy Gallagher, was permitted to sever his connexion with the Club he had served so well for fourteen years.

Then followed a period which, so far as League honours were concerned, had never been so lean—for nine years we failed to win the Championship, although we were never very far away.

Many fine young players became attached to Celtic during that period, and it seemed as if a blight had been cast over the team with regard to the League.

John Thomson, John M'Menemy, Willie M'Gonagle were the recruits of 1926–27 who were later to gain fame, and two years later Charley Geatons came from Lochgelly Celtic to join brother Fifers.

The following season, 1929–30, saw, among others, Peter Scarff, Charley Napier and Bertie Thomson jump into the limelight, followed a year later by Willie Cook, John Morrison, Hugh Smith, Joe Cowan, &c.

Still the Flag eluded us. In game after game, despite the strenuous efforts and often brilliantly superior play of our men, things went wrong in some mysterious manner.

Our cup of sorrow and misfortune was filled to over-flowing when our great goalkeeper, John Thomson, met with a regrettable accident at Ibrox Park on 5th September, 1931, which caused his untimely death.

The shock had a tremendous effect on our players, one which we firmly believe was responsible for many failures during the next few years.

The team was playing first-class football when the blow fell, and continued to do so, but without any great fire or enthusiasm; it seemed as if they had lost heart.

Nor did fortune cease to frown upon them. Injury followed injury in almost fiendish fashion, and when Peter Scarff, whose health had been bad for a year or more, died 9th December, 1933, we seemed doomed to continual misfortune.

But the work of building still went on. Joe Kennaway had come from Canada to succeed John Thomson; Bobby Hogg, Frank, and later Hugh O'Donnell, then Willie Buchan, Johnny Crum, Malcolm M'Donald and George Paterson came along to infuse a new spirit into our jaded and disappointed team.

Still things failed to improve, although we had the satisfaction of finishing second to Rangers in 1934–35, this being our best since four years earlier.

At the end of this season the Directors, confident that in their alliance team they had youngsters due to take their places in the first team, transferred the brothers O'Donnell and Charley Napier—Peter Wilson and Alec and Bertie Thomson had already gone.

It was significant of the number of changes in the personnel of the team that of the lot that won the cup in 1931 only M'Gonagle, Geatons and M'Grory remained, and yet in five seasons a new combination had been brought together which promised to open up a new era for the Club. Frank Murphy and Jimmy Delaney had forced their way into the League team, George Paterson was now recognized as a first-class half-back—he came as a centre-forward—and Willie Lyon had left Hampden Park to join a club he was to captain in a great revival.

And so in 1935–36, after wandering in the League wilderness for ten weary years, we regained the title of Champions with a total only once surpassed in a competition of similiar size, and that by one point only.

It was not accomplished easily either—our old friend (?) " Mr. Injury " was often in evidence—but a new spirit was abroad and the management felt that their years of worry and careful search had at last met with reward.

The work of the team, inspired by the leadership of James M'Grory and splendidly captained by Willie Lyon, gave promise of better days and made me feel that the old Celtic spirit, which was believed to have died out, was reborn to emulate the deeds of famous predecessors.

Perhaps it was too much to expect that after such a strenuous season, during which the players had suffered many serious injuries, they could retain the Championship in 1936–37.

But for M'Grory's misfortune at the beginning of the season in suffering from knee injury which deprived us of his services for a number of games, and a similar misfortune to Delaney, we might easily have accomplished the feat, but it was too much and we had to be content with other prizes dealt with elsewhere.

Despite the success which was now regularly coming our way, recruiting was still being carried on.

Jimmy M'Stay, Wilson and M'Gonagle were allowed to go elsewhere in order to make room for the youngsters who were developing, and who had to be considered.

Our season did not open in too promising a manner, as we lost four points in our first four games and fell to Rangers a fortnight later.

At the beginning of October we were beaten at Arbroath—we had 11 points for 11 games at this stage—but the team had gradually been finding its feet, and from 9th October, 1937, until 2nd April, 1938, they maintained an unbeaten run and so laid the foundation of the Club's nineteenth Championship.

Two draws in March and a defeat on 2nd April at Falkirk gave some of our opponents the idea that the boys were cracking up, and that the Championship would slip through their fingers, but three sound victories in our concluding games made victory certain.

The transfer of Willie Buchan to Blackpool in November was thought to be a mistake on the part of the management, but with their characteristic foresight they introduced a new inside formation—Jimmy M'Grory having shown that *anno Domini* was affecting his play.

Accordingly Crum took over the leadership with

M'Donald at inside right and Divers at inside left, and almost immediately a game on the lines of the good old days was struck.

Suffice to say that the Flag was won with the occasional assistance of a few reserve players, but it is worthy of notice that the attack was practically that of our alliance team two years earlier—another tribute to the judgment and ability of those responsible for keeping up the supply.

The season just ended has therefore again proved the wisdom and care with which the Club has been controlled during its fifty years' existence, and the name of Celtic is to-day, as it was in the beginning, synonymous with enterprise and progress.

Youth will be served they say; the last season has proved this beyond all doubt, as to-day we possess one of the youngest teams in the League and almost entirely composed of lads who have served their apprenticeship in our Alliance team.

JOHN SHAUGHNESSY, J.P.
Director, 1911 to date

JOHN McKILLOP
Director, 1921 to date

ROBERT KELLY
Director, 1931 to date

1892

Top row: Jerry Reynolds, Joe Cullen, and Dan Doyle

Second row: W. Maley, J. Kelly, and P. Gallacher

Third row: N. McCallum, Alex. Brady, J. Madden, Alex. McMahon, and J. Campbell

BOARD OF DIRECTORS, 1907

1896

Top row: T. Maguire (Trainer), J. Kelly, Alan Martin, D. Doyle, B. Battles, and W. Ferguson

2nd row: J. Madden, A. McMahon, P. Meechan, and W. Maley

3rd row: J. Blessington, Glasgow Cup, and D. McArthur

P. GALLAGHER

J. McSTAY

J. McGRORY

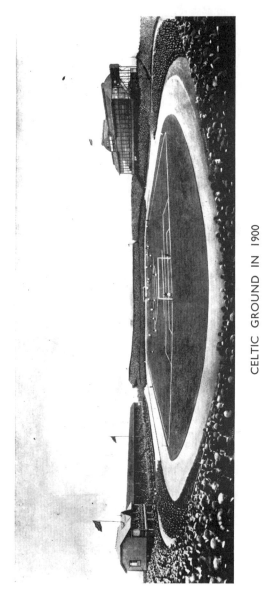

CELTIC GROUND IN 1900

With ground specially seated for the now famous Rosebery International

JAMES QUINN

ALEC McNAIR

JAMES YOUNG

J. McMENEMY

1897

Top row: J. Curran, D. McArthur, J. Blessington, J. Cullen, T. Bonnar (Trainer), T. Dunbar, J. Campbell, J. Reynolds, and P. Gallacher

2nd row: Joe Cassidy, J. Madden, J. Kelly, D. Doyle, and W. Maley

3rd row: J. Divers, A. McMahon, and C. McEleny

Athletics

THE Celtic Club have an indisputable claim to be the pioneers of athletic sports on a really grand scale, their enterprise giving athletics a new lease of life which developed to such an extent that the summer gatherings attracted attendances far beyond the wildest dreams of club promoters.

The first Celtic sports meeting held on the old ground in 1890 was on a very modest scale, one Saturday being devoted to confined events and the next to open events.

The attendances were small, and no doubt owing to the primitive nature of the track only three competitors took part in the cycling events—R. A. Vogt and the brothers Kirkwood of Paisley.

When the Club removed to the new and present ground the sports were continued, and on the occasion of the first meeting there an innovation, which was later to be developed on a magnificent scale, was introduced in the presence of competitors from England and Ireland.

To Sonny Morton, 4 and 10 miles champion of England; J. Kibblewhite, 1 mile champion; E. W. Parry, cross-country champion; and D. D. Bulger, Irish 100 yards and hurdle champion, belong the honour of being the first of a long list of " foreign " competitors at Celtic sports—thus setting a fashion which was continued as long as the Club preserved the continuity of their great gatherings and imitated by others up to the present.

Following the athletes I have named came that great English sprint champion and sportsman Charley Bradley, Fred Bacon, George Crossland, Harry Watkins, Max Wittenburg, Godfrey Shaw, and later on Alf Shrubb, Sid Thomas, W. E. Applegarth, R. E. Walker and many others.

The Celtic Club was the first to introduce American athletes to Scotland, and those great meetings graced by the presence of Arthur Duffy, Melvin Sheppard, Maxwell Long, Tewkesbury, J. J. Flanagan the mighty, and O. Kraeuslein, the famous hurdler, will never be forgotten by those who were privileged to be present.

Famous Irish athletes who followed Dan Bulger with unfailing regularity in their attendance at Celtic sports included that great ball putter genial Denis Horgan; the brothers Con and Pat Leahy, the famous high jumpers from Cork; P. J. O'Connor, for many years record holder of the long jump; Denis and Willie Murray the sprinter; T. F. Kiely, the hammer thrower; and M'Kenzie, Finnigan, Mullen, I. M. Donovan and many other track champions.

Until the alteration in the date of opening the football season, which wiped out the use of the second Saturday in August, the date on which the meetings were always held, the Celtic Club's sports were regarded as the principal meeting in Scotland and attracted athletes from practically all parts of the world; indeed to win a " Celtic handicap " was the ambition of every runner in those days.

The Celtic Club has, throughout its fifty years, displayed a desire amounting to almost anxiety to provide entertainment for the public.

Many years ago opportunities were provided to try and interest the public of Glasgow in the game of baseball, and on more than one occasion the Irish game of hurling was played.

Professional running was given an innings, and the cream of athletes in that category were induced by means of generous cash prizes to play their part in making the meetings a success.

Unfortunately the Club's efforts were not appreciated, the public being unwilling to patronize a sport in which the " efforts " of the runners were too obvious, and so the experiment was abandoned.

Dirt track racing, given a good trial, also failed to catch on, but the fact remains that Celtic proved their willingness to provide any kind of sport so long as the public showed its desire to witness it.

Cycling

THE rise and fall in the popularity of track cycling and its connexion with Celtic Park deserves, nay demands, a chapter all to itself.

I referred to the primitive track of the original ground; its faults were duly noted when the new ground was being prepared, with the result that a special track was laid down for that branch of sport.

The red cinder track at Celtic Park was the scene of many great struggles among our Scottish cyclists, and on its surface were ridden countless close finishes in which Vogt, M'Laren, Woods, Killachy, Alexander, M'Farlane, Ross, Peat, Silver, Torrance, Dan Flynn, Brownlie, M'Neil and others participated.

The popularity of cycling increased by leaps and bounds, and with their wonted enterprise the Directors (the Club was now a Limited Company) decided to give the sport every encouragement and built a cement track, the first of its kind in Scotland.

The innovation was appreciated to such an extent that the crowds flocked to witness the prowess of champions from all quarters of the globe.

The Glasgow Merchants' Cycling Club at that period, a most enterprising and flourishing body, fired by the assistance and encouragement given them at Parkhead, promoted several great meetings, and the result was that every champion of note appeared at Parkhead.

For the first and only occasion in history, the World's Cycling Championships were held in Scotland and at Celtic Park in 1898, and the scenes during this great festival will never be forgotten.

Champions from all parts of the world competed— Willy Arends, Zimmerman, Bourillion, Barden, Platt Betts, Ben Jones, Gascoigne—the public went simply mad on the sport around the end of the last century and the beginning of the present.

But alas! its very popularity proved its undoing. The cyclists failed to maintain the standard from various causes; the " makers amateur " type assisting in the downfall which was completed by the influence of the " bookie ".

The famous track, round which the cream of the world's athletes had raced, fell into almost disuse, unless at the Club's sports when Harry Martin, that intrepid motor-cyclist, introduced the more modern type of machine and thrilled the large crowds with his record-breaking feats in a still atmosphere which was rent by the plaudits of many thousands as the finishing gun was heard. Here, too, A. E. Wick set up British record for motor-paced mile, going round at the rate of 54 miles per hour.

And so in 1914 the cement track was broken up and the space devoted to the ever-increasing demands of football crowds.

Cycling is on the boom once more, and the Celtic Club at the comparatively modest meeting they hold nowadays have given it every encouragement, but we old-timers cannot help sighing as we recall the days when Celtic sports, with its galaxy of champions—track, field and cycling—were events anticipated and enjoyed as the greatest of the year.

" Milestones "

IN the big list of important games which follows, my readers may wonder why Cup Ties predominate to such an extent.

I think it will readily be understood that the Celtic's first year brought them right into the " high spots " by reason of the work of their team in the Cup Ties.

Most of our team had been " blooded ", so to speak, by the very stern and ungenerous opposition accorded to them in the ties of the Exhibition Cup of 1888, and when they had to face up to the competitions for the Scottish and Glasgow Cups they were imbued with a desire to make up for their fall in the Exhibition tourney.

Right away we were called upon to face Cowlairs, our conquerors in the Exhibition Final, and right well did we avenge that undeserved defeat. Cowlairs had been specially strengthened in this tie by the inclusion of Bob Kelso, brought specially down from Newcastle for the " slaughter ", but our lot gave a display that had never been equalled for dash and precision in the history of the game. We won by 8-0, and Celtic came right into the front lines at once.

We disposed of Albion Rovers and St. Bernards in the next two rounds, and were then called upon to meet our local rivals, Clyde, at Celtic Park in the fifth round.

On a day of rain, with a ground absolutely water-logged, we lost by 1–0 after a wonderful display by Clyde's goalie, W. Chalmers, but on the advice of many prominent officials who were present (it is to be remembered we were still novices as far as legislative work was concerned), we protested on the unplayability of the ground, in which we were supported by the referee, and the tie was ordered to be replayed.

A week later we dismissed Clyde by 9–2, proceeding to Falkirk to meet East Stirlingshire in the sixth round, an unforgettable match in which our opponents snatched a goal lead early in the game and then packed their goal.

Until within five minutes of the end, play raged entirely round the home goal. There were no nets in those days, and the goalkeeper wore the same jersey as his colleagues, and no one will ever be able to say how many goals were stopped by arms belonging to others than the goalie; but all came right in the end when our lot scored two quick goals to pull the tie out of the fire.

We travelled to Dumbarton to play the semi-final, to meet the then famous Sons of the Rock, who in those days were a power in the land and especially so on what was then termed " Fatal Boghead ".

Included in Dumbarton's team that day was John Madden, who had agreed to play for us that season but " deserted " at the last moment, and was playing then at the top of his form at outside right for his home town.

The feeling amongst the Dumbarton supporters was intensified by the inclusion in the Celtic team of McLaren and Groves, late of the Hibernians, who two years before had helped materially to defeat Dumbarton in the Scottish Final at Hampden Park.

To my mind Celtic that day laid the foundation of their great form in Cup Ties which has been so prominent down the years. Against a side which spared neither themselves nor their opponents, the Green and White brigade took everything in their stride and ran out winners by 4–1 in a game which is still spoken of down Levenside way by many of the old-timers.

It would be difficult to imagine the feelings of the members of the Celtic Club, officials, players and others on that wintry February morning, when they began to realize that the great day had arrived.

History had been made, of that there was no doubt. To reach the Final of the Scottish Cup after an existence of only a few months was in itself a feat unheard of— aye, even undreamt of, but the fact remained that in the afternoon they were to fight for the blue riband of Scottish football.

Pride to an excessive extent undoubtedly filled the hearts of all connected with the new Club, but particularly in the breasts of the enthusiastic founders— the pioneers, so to speak—was there a feeling of complete satisfaction.

Elsewhere it has been stated that very few of the committee possessed any real knowledge or experience of football, although no doubt quite a number believed that their year's connexion with it entitled them to believe they did.

The experienced members, however, had no delusions regarding the task in hand, despite the presence of several tried players in their ranks, and possibly it was with a feeling of trepidation that they proceeded Hampden-wards, as after all the trial was a tremendous one.

The forenoon was most depressing. A high wind sent the snow swirling around, and at eleven o'clock there was a thin coating on the turf.

The S.F.A. officials were on the scene, and after inspecting the ground decided that there was nothing to prevent the game from proceeding—a reasonable enough conclusion.

The Weather Clerk, however, had other ideas. The gale increased in fury, and the thin covering of snow became a thick carpet—between two and three o'clock there was a blinding snowstorm.

The decision having been arrived at, however, there was nothing to be done but open the gates, and despite the elements the crowds swarmed in to fill the ground, with the snow sweeping the length of the field.

The *Glasgow Herald*, commenting on the conditions, stated that everyone was agreed on the inadvisability of settling so important a match on such a ground, but the die was cast.

Inside the pavilion, the Association hurriedly held a meeting, at which it was decided that, notwithstanding the ground was by this time unplayable, the tie should be played.

Both teams played under protest, and it was understood by all the men that a friendly game was being played.

Previous to the start of the game much hilarity was caused by the players indulging in a snowballing battle, but quickly the more serious business was tackled.

Friendly or no friendly, both sides were keen to win, and let it be said that never was there a greater test of endurance entered into with such enthusiasm.

Celtic won the toss and naturally decided to play with the wind, with the result that Third's defence was sorely tried. But first let me give the names of the heroes of this great struggle.

CELTIC: John Kelly; Gallacher and M'Keown; W. Maley, James Kelly and M'Laren; M'Callum, Dunbar, Groves, Coleman and T. E. Maley.

3RD L.R.V.: Downie; A. Thomson and Rae; M'Farlane, Auld and Lochhead; Marshall, Oswald, junr., Oswald, senr., Johnstone and Hannah.

Referee: Mr. C. Campbell, V.P., S.F.A.

Umpires: T. Park, Cambuslang; R. Harrison, Kilmarnock.

Celtic's play was marvellous during the early stages, their passing being almost perfect, considering the ground conditions; but they soon realized that it was one thing to get near the goal and another to score.

Downie in the Volunteers' goal seemed to be inspired, saving ball after ball in a manner which surprised even his greatest admirers.

For over a quarter of an hour Third were kept on the defensive, with the exception of a couple of fruitless but plucky raids by Johnny Marshall—who, it is worth recalling, afterwards became a famous referee.

Then at twenty minutes the blow fell. Downie had just brought off another magnificent save and the ball was sent up the left to Johnstone, who sped away and crossed, for Marshall to score!

A well-taken goal, but entirely against the play, and all the time the ball was becoming heavier and of course less easy to propel.

Disregarding the set-back, Celtic continued to serve up wonderful football, only to find Downie in unbelievable form. His saving bordered on the miraculous on many occasions, and Third crossed over very lucky leaders by 1—0.

With the gale behind them in the second half, the Volunteers were a different proposition, especially as they held the goal lead.

All the time, be it remembered, the snow was falling, and some of the players were showing signs of exhaustion.

Still they fought on doggedly, Third to hold and if possible increase their lead, and Celtic to wipe it out—a magnificent struggle and an admirable exhibition of football and physical endurance.

The Volunteers had more of the game now, but Celts' raids were fraught with danger to Downie and his co-defenders.

One beautiful advance in which the five Celtic forwards participated ended in the ball being sent past when a goal seemed certain, and their prospects of success faded out completely when John Kelly's frozen hands failed to hold a shot from Oswald, junr., some twenty minutes from the end.

Facing the snow and wintry wind two goals in arrears took the heart out of the hitherto dominant Celts, and Third, now on the highroad to victory, finished on a confident note, Hannah adding a third goal in the last minute of the game.

It goes without saying that, following the " snow " game, there was considerable discussion as to whether the result would stand.

At the S.F.A. meeting it transpired, although there was no secret about it, that the officials had, previous to the game, given instructions that both teams should play under protest. Indeed, both had actually intimated their objections to the conditions.

The referee and the two umpires were questioned, and having stated that in their opinion the ground was unplayable, the Association decided that the game should be replayed on the following Saturday.

The conditions on this occasion were fairly good, the only fault to be found being that the surface was very hard owing to frost.

3rd Lanark, having claimed that the previous game should stand, despite their agreement to protest against the ground conditions, now performed a rather comical *volte-face* by intimating a protest against the ground in the replay, owing to its hard condition—and they also protested against the Association's decision!

On this occasion they won the toss and took advantage of a fairly strong breeze, starting off in storming fashion, but Celts' defence was solid, and soon the Parkhead attack was hammering at Downie's goal.

M'Callum quickly smashed one past the Volunteers' goalkeeper, but offside had sounded. The crowd were seething with excitement as play raged from end to end, both defences being exceptionally solid.

Willie Groves received a tremendous cheer for a mazy run, during which he travelled nearly the length of the field, his final pass being intercepted by Andrew Thomson. Johnny Coleman was injured and taken off, but Celtic were not to be denied. M'Callum sent along a terrific shot which appeared to have Downie beaten, the upright intervening to save the situation for the Volunteers.

Coleman returned to shoot past in a hot attack, and then Third's left wing started a dangerous movement, which looked like bearing fruit when Gallacher miskicked, but James Kelly saved the situation with a timely intervention.

Third, keeping up the pressure, gave the Celtic defence some anxious moments. Marshall sent in a stiff shot which Kelly cleared, but they claimed that the ball had crossed the line.

Mr. Charley Campbell consulted with his umpires and upheld their claim, which gave them the lead after twenty-three minutes' play.

Some beautiful combination by the Celtic forwards ended in M'Callum being presented with an excellent opportunity of squaring matters, which, unfortunately for Celtic, was not accepted, and they crossed over a goal behind.

On the resumption Downie displayed magnificent saving ability when Celts attacked strongly. He alone prevented them from equalizing, and in addition the Volunteers' forwards were unable to move, so firm was the grip on them by their opponents' half-backs.

Unfortunately for Celtic their shooting was not on a par with their outfield play, and many glorious opportunities were squandered.

Still, such continuous pressure could not fail to bring

reward and at last, in twenty-two minutes, the teams were level when M'Callum headed past the hitherto unbeatable Downie.

Celtic were now masters of the situation in all but goals. Probably they concentrated too much on attack, as a sudden dash upfield by Third presented Oswald with an opening which was promptly seized, and the Volunteers were once more on the lead.

Celtic made frantic efforts to save the tie, but the Cathkin defence held out until the end, to win the cup for the first time in their history.

And so Celtic's first bid to gain the trophy ended in failure, but what a glorious failure! They had astonished the football world by reaching the final in their first year, and even in defeat had given an exhibition seldom if ever equalled, one which in the years to come was to be re-garded as their own particular brand of football and of the most scientific order.

Season 1890-91 saw Celtic win their first major trophy, and their success was all the more welcome as in the final they had the satisfaction of defeating the team which had given them their first cup defeat.

The Glasgow Cup was a fairly new competition, being instituted three years previously. Cambuslang had won it by beating Rangers in 1887-88. Queen's Park were successful at the expense of Partick Thistle a year later, and in 1889-90 the Amateurs had beaten Celtic by 3-2.

In the fourth year of the competition. Celtic and 3rd Lanark fielded the following teams, both of which dif-fered considerably from those of the Scottish Final of 1889.

D

CELTIC: Bell; Reynolds and M'Keown; Gallacher, Kelly and W. Maley; Madden, Boyle, Dowds, Dunbar and Campbell.

3RD LANARK: Downie; A. Thomson and Smith; Scott, Love and Lochhead; Lapsley, W. Thomson, Johnstone, M'Innes and Burke.

Referee: Mr. Watson, Dundee.

Umpires: Mr. Bishop, Falkirk; Mr. Mackay, Campsie.

The Volunteers started off with a rush, to find Bell ready and willing, and very soon Celts were on the attack, Madden and Boyle giving the opposition plenty of running to keep them from going through.

Andrew Thomson had his hands full with Dunbar and Campbell, who had been recruited from Benburb. Indeed the back was on many occasions forced to kick out for safety, a most unusual proceeding on his part, as he was a delightful kicker and invariably placed the ball to his forwards with great accuracy.

Downie was again prominent, saving a long shot from the Celtic left-half just as it was passing under the bar.

The Volunteers, however, were persistent and Jerry Reynolds' head came in useful several times. Celtic indulged in a lovely forward movement which ought to have brought a goal, Downie bringing off a fine save when all seemed lost.

Midway through the first half Celtic went ahead, although not in a very convincing manner. Campbell sent over a high ball, which rebounded from the post, and Lochhead in attempting to clear headed through his own goal.

Smith, the Cathkin back, came up and sent a huge punt

into goal, which Bell stopped with difficulty, but Celts were now full of confidence and with Madden and Dowds in brilliant form, ably backed up by three aggressive half-backs, they had their opponents in sad straits.

The Volunteers started the second half by scoring through Lapsley, who, however, was given offside. They fought back splendidly, although it was evident that they were not just good enough for their more mobile opponents.

Jimmy Kelly broke through and forced Thomson to concede a corner from which Peter Dowds scored, and continuing to dominate the game, Campbell added a third.

Their opponents were by no means beaten yet, however, and Billy Love, this sterling little half-back from Thornliebank, had a magnificent effort saved by Bell.

Madden got another past Downie which was disallowed—it was all Celtic now and before the end Campbell added the fourth to give Celtic a convincing victory and their first big cup.

A very clever band of reserve players were gathered together in that season, who practically carried all before them—their record for the season reads as follows:

Played, 37 games. Won, 31. Drawn, 6. Lost, 0. Goals for, 187. Goals against, 32.

They won the Scottish Second Eleven Cup by the record score of 13 goals to 1, their victims being St. Mirren, who, by the way, were first to score.

Our team on this record-making occasion was as follows: M. Dolan; Collins and T. Dunbar; T. Murray, F. Dolan and Kyle; Cunningham, Devlin, Coleman, Foran and M'Greachan.

There was some hefty scoring in the rounds leading up to the Final, Battlefield being defeated by 10–0; Northern, 9–0; St. Johnstone, 12–1; Royal Albert, 6–0; Morton, 4–3; and Heart of Midlothian in the Semi-Final by 4–2.

The League results during the early months of 1891–92 gave no indication that the season was to be a memorable one in the history of the new Club by the establishment of a record which was not equalled for sixteen seasons—the winning of the three cups.

Clyde, making their first appearance in the final of the Glasgow Cup, were not expected to supply very serious opposition, although in their ranks they possessed some first-class players; among them was Jimmy M'Laren, the " Ould Giniral ", who had dropped out of the Celtic team after a short but particularly useful three years.

The game was played at Cathkin Park under miserable conditions—the rain descending in torrents unceasingly throughout the game.

The teams lined up as follows:

CELTIC: Duff; Reynolds and Doyle; Dowds, Kelly and W. Maley; M'Callum, Brady, Madden, M'Mahon and Campbell.

CLYDE: Fortune; Sawers and Maxwell; Bowie, Cherrie and M'Laren; M'Intosh, Harvey, W. Sawers, Johnstone and M'Innes.

Referee: Mr. Hay, Dumfries.

Play was fairly even to begin with, as although the Celtic forwards were often in their opponents' territory, the Clyde backs, by no means particular regarding their methods, broke up many dangerous attacks.

Possibly the more ornate play of the Parkhead forwards made them easy victims, as victims they were, numerous free kicks being awarded, but these failed to bring any tangible reward.

Clyde, however, and perhaps more wisely, depended on direct and often erratic attack which, backed up with any amount of pluck and enthusiasm, managed to hold out until twenty minutes had elapsed, when M'Callum drew first blood.

Ten minutes later his partner, Alec Brady, added a second and two very " drookit " teams retired at the interval with Celts leading by 2–0.

Clyde's resumption was as successful as it was un-expected. Bowie with a long raking shot beat Duff all ends up in two minutes, and for a time the Brigtonians actually dominated the play.

As Clyde improved Celts went from bad to worse, and it actually seemed as if they were going to fall to pieces, especially when Brady missed an open goal.

This state of affairs continued for about twenty minutes and then the game took another swing, one which was to create havoc in the Clyde camp.

In a desperate assault M'Mahon put Celtic two ahead once more, and simply sweeping through all opposition Kelly and Madden increased the score to five.

Clyde strove frantically to stem the now practically irresistible Celtic tide, but their efforts were of no avail, and Johnny Campbell scoring twice in the closing minutes put the finishing touch on Celtic's second suc-cessive victory in the competition, and laid the first stone in the never-to-be-forgotten three-cup edifice.

Four months later Celtic found themselves for the second time in their short life of four seasons in the final of the Scottish Cup, their opponents on this occasion being Queen's Park, who two years before had beaten them in both Glasgow and Scottish Cup competitions.

In order to give some idea of the tremendous interest which was manifested in the event, the description of the scenes previous to the game given in the *Glasgow Herald* on the following Monday is worth reprinting.

" This game will long be remembered in the annals of football for the enthusiasm it aroused.

" Nothing else had been talked about since it became known that Queen's Park and Celtic were to meet.

" There were close on 40,000 present, and Rangers had made special preparations at Ibrox by erecting two new stands and additional terracing.

" The scenes on the way to the field will long be remembered, in fact there was never anything approaching it in the history of the game.

" As early as noon—four hours before the time of starting—people began to wend their way towards Ibrox, and by 2 o'clock the ground was packed.

" Thirteen special trains and several ordinary arrived at Ibrox Station by 3 o'clock, and the pressure at the gates was so great that it was decided to close them.

" Under Capt. Hamilton over 100 constables were on duty besides four on horseback, but the crowd was a good-natured one and passed the time singing popular airs.

" An hour before the kick-off the pressure on the

terracing was so great that the crowd invaded the field of play. The strenuous and tactful efforts of the police, however, managed to restore something like order."

Such were the conditions under which Celtic made their second appearance in the Final and against the then mighty Queen's Park, who had on eight occasions appeared in the event to prove successful each time.

The Amateurs' friends and others were perhaps naturally enough in the great majority and were very disappointed when it was learned that Walter Arnott was unable to play owing to injury, but J. Gillespie was introduced from Falkirk at right-half, thus permitting Donald Sillars to step into Arnott's position.

CELTIC: Cullen; Reynolds and Doyle; W. Maley, Kelly and Dowds; M'Callum, Brady, Madden, M'Mahon and Campbell.

QUEEN'S PARK: Baird; Sillars and Smellie; Gillespie, Robertson and Stewart; Gullilland, Waddell, Hamilton, Lambie and Sellar.

Referee: Mr. George Sneddon, President of the S.F.A.

The ground was rather soft and was expected to cut up badly. Early raids by Bill Sellar looked ominous for Celtic, but by degrees their forwards got going, and Smellie's leg prevented M'Callum from scoring from Campbell's cross.

The footing was treacherous, but despite this the M'Mahon-Campbell wing was functioning with the most beautiful precision, and it was believed that from that side would come the fireworks.

Queen's, inspired by Tom Robertson, a tremendous worker, were trying desperately to establish a lead, and

Cullen's charge ran many narrow escapes, but Queen's goal was quite as often in danger when Celts' forwards were in the vicinity.

Needless to say, the crowds were seething with excitement, so much so that, owing to encroachment on the playing pitch, the game had to be stopped for several minutes to allow it to be cleared.

Quickly the teams were at it again, hammer and tongs; all the time the spectators were shouting themselves hoarse as each goal in turn had hairbreadth escapes.

Altering their tactics, Doyle and Kelly attempted to beat Baird with long drooping shots, but the Ayrshire goalkeeper was safe as the bank.

In the closing minutes of the first half he did particularly good work while Celts pressed strongly in order to snatch a lead, and so the teams retired goalless.

A slip by Bob Smellie immediately after the restart almost let the eager Celts in on Baird, but Sillars saved the situation with a magnificent tackle.

Not to be denied Celtic pressed fiercely, and at the end of fifteen minutes had the satisfaction of gaining the lead.

Madden contributed to this success by shooting strongly. Baird with a great leap stopped the shot but fell, and the ball going out to Campbell, the outside left had no difficulty in scoring.

The excitement was terrific, but the crowd were almost hysterical when a minute later Queen's squeezed the ball past Joe Cullen, seconds after the whistle had sounded for offside.

The rest of the game was fought out at a furious pace, despite the heavy going, the Amateurs trying every wile to elude the Celtic defenders, but Doyle and Reynolds were impregnable.

The game ended 1–0 in favour of Celtic, but they had not yet won the cup as it transpired that at the interval it had been agreed to play a friendly.

In the evening the S.F.A. committee had a meeting and decided that the clubs should meet again on 9th April and that the admission charge should be doubled.

The doubling of the charge for admission certainly kept down the attendance, as it numbered 22,000, although it was stated that the beautiful weather which was enjoyed on this occasion took many people, who otherwise would have gone to Ibrox, out of town.

Madden was unable to turn out for Celtic, Queen's being similarly handicapped by the absence of Bob Smellie. Dowds led the Celtic attack and Sellar stepped back to Smellie's position.

With the wind behind them Queen's harassed the Celtic defenders for some time, Cullen, Reynolds and Doyle being often sorely tried to keep out their opponents.

The Amateurs undoubtedly had the better of the first half and thoroughly deserved the lead with a well-taken goal by Tommy Waddell, their indefatigable inside right.

When Celts came out after the interval they wore a grim and determined look, and it was obvious that they meant business.

In their opening rush they almost scored, and with M'Mahon and Campbell serving up some delightful football the crowd often found themselves compelled to applaud, although their sympathies clearly lay elsewhere.

It was not surprising therefore that Campbell equalized

D 2

in five minutes. Continuing to display delightful combination the Celtic forwards and half-backs overwhelmed
their opponents, and Campbell added a second goal to
give them the lead at last.

Although Queen's were passing through a bad time
and showed signs of collapse, Jimmy Hamilton their
sturdy leader never gave in. Single-handed he attempted
on many occasions to force his way past Reynolds and
Doyle but found them steady as rocks.

Doyle indeed was often up lifting beautifully timed
balls into Queen's goal—once Dowds with an overhead
kick almost added the third.

With the cup as good as won Celts eased off, and
Queen's made a dying but unavailing effort to level the
scores, and then M'Mahon, indulging in one of those
mazy runs—head down arms outstretched—simply walked
through the Amateurs' defence to register the third goal.

Queen's became demoralized and one of their defenders put through his own goal, M'Mahon completing
their downfall by heading the fifth from a corner kick.

The Glasgow Charity Cup Final of 1892 was to have
a special significance in view of subsequent events, as it
was the first occasion on which the two clubs, afterwards
to become the greatest rivals football has ever known,
had met in the final of any cup.

The feelings of the Celtic players and officials previous
to this game may easily be imagined—they had already
won the Glasgow Cup and the Scottish Cup: would
they on this memorable day create a record hitherto
undreamt of by winning the third important trophy in
the one season?

WILLIAM McKILLOP, M.P.
Hon. President, 1893–4–5–6

THOMAS WHITE, B.L.

Director from 1908 to date
Chairman since 1914

1898

Top row: D. Friel (Trainer), R. Davidson, Alick King, Manager Maley, Willie Orr, John Hodge, and Tom Hynds

2nd row: D. Storrier, B. Battles, H. Goldie, J. Welford, D. Doyle, J. Campbell, A. McMahon, and P. Gilhooly

3rd row: J. Fisher, Dan McArthur, and Jack Bell

1901

Back row: B. Battles, W. Loney, H. Marshall, J. Moir, A. McMahon, H. Watson, John Campbell, W. Orr, A. McPherson, D. McLeod, and P. Somers

2nd row: J. Quinn, J. McMenemy, W. McCaffrey, Manager Maley, A. Crawford, T. McDermott, and D. Hamilton

Exhibition Cup in centre

1908

WINNERS OF SCOTTISH, GLASGOW, GLASGOW CHARITY
CUPS AND SCOTTISH LEAGUE CHAMPIONSHIP

Top row: Directors, Tom White, J. Kelly, Tom Colgan, John McKillop,
James Grant, and M. Dunbar

2nd row: Manager Maley, J. Young, P. Somers, J. McMenemy, D. Adams,
J. Mitchell, J. Weir, and R. Davis (Trainer)

3rd row: D. Hamilton, D. McLeod, W. Loney, J. Hay, J. Quinn, and
Alex McNair

Charity, Scottish and Glasgow Cups in centre

1912

Back row: Directors M. Dunbar, J. Shaughnessy,
J. McKillop, T. Colgan

2nd row: W. Quinn (Trainer), W. Loney, J. McMenemy, J. Dodds,
J. Quinn, P. Johnstone, J. Young, W. Maley (Manager)

Front row: A. McAtee, J. Browning, J. Kelly (Chairman), P. Gallagher,
T. McGregor, A. McNair

1923

Top row, left to right: Ed. McGarvey (Asst. Trainer), A. McNair,
W. McStay, C. Shaw, Hugh Hilley, W. Maley (Manager), J. McStay,
J. McFarlane, and W. Quinn (Trainer)

2nd row, left to right: A. McAtee, J. Cassidy, A. McLean, W. Cringan,
P. Gallagher, and P. Connolly

Scottish Cup in centre

1925

Top row: W. Maley, Manager; W. McStay, P. Shevlin, H. Hilley, and Mr. Tom White, Chairman

2nd row: P. Wilson, J. McStay, J. McFarlane, A. McLean

3rd row: P. Connolly, P. Gallagher, J. McGrory, and A. Thomson

Scottish Cup in centre

Record holders 1925 with 11 wins

THOMAS COLGAN

Club's Senior Director.   On Board from 1904 to date

PRESENT BOARD OF DIRECTORS

1931

Top row: W. Maley, Manager; C. Geatons, W .Cook, John Thomson, W. McGonagle, P. Wilson, W. Quinn (Trainer)
2nd row: C. Napier, P. Scarff, J. McGrory, J. McStay, R. Thomson, and A. Thomson. Scottish Cup in centre

Record win in Scottish Cup 13 times, when defeating Motherwell after a replay

Dowds was unfortunately not available and the veteran Paddy Gallacher came in at left-half, otherwise the team was on the usual lines.

Here are the names of the players who took part in the memorable battle—what memories they bring back.

CELTIC: Cullen; Reynolds and Doyle; W. Maley, Kelly and Gallacher; M'Callum, Brady, Madden, M'Mahon and Campbell.

RANGERS: Haddow; Donald Gow and Dunbar; Marshall, A. M'Creadie and Muir; Kerr, M'Innes (Notts County), Gibb, Turnbull and M'Pherson.

Referee: Mr. T. Park, Cambuslang.

Heavy rain had fallen during the week and the ground was in consequence very soft, but the crowds rolled up in great numbers certain that they would witness a tremendously keen game.

M'Pherson and Turnbull caused Reynolds endless trouble during the opening minutes, but Jerry ultimately succeeded in beating them back, and M'Mahon and Campbell, Celts' wizard left-wing pair, began to demand attention. Their clever advances failed to produce any fruit, however, as poor use was made of Campbell's perfect crosses, although as the game wore on Haddow was more frequently called upon and was cheered on many occasions for his splendid goalkeeping.

Rangers, rather against the run of play, were presented with an opportunity to take the lead, but M'Pherson failed to accept and play was immediately transferred to the other end, where Haddow again and again saved apparently certain goals.

His display inspired his colleagues, who showed improvement, and they actually got the ball past Cullen, but Mr. Park disallowed the point for offside.

M'Innes and Kerr now took the eye with some inter-passing which compared favourably with Celts' left-wing pair. Neither side could score, however, and the teams crossed over as they had started, although the play had been exceptionally fast and clever and had kept the spectators in a state of great excitement.

The beginning of the second half saw Donald Gow hard pressed by Campbell and M'Mahon — the bouts were most enjoyable and honours were fairly well divided.

Sandy M'Mahon, however, was a crafty player. Realiz-ing that direct methods were not going to be profitable against such a tactician as Gow, he wandered over to the right and getting the defenders where he wanted them suddenly screwed the ball over to Campbell who, lying unmarked, headed past Haddow fifteen minutes after the restart.

Celts were now dominant but Rangers contested every inch and some marvellous football was seen. Try as they would Celtic could not increase their lead, while their opponents found a resolute middle line holding their forwards in a firm grip.

Ten minutes from the end M'Callum scored to dis-cover that Mr. Park had other ideas, but putting on full steam Celts increased their lead when Campbell again headed through, this time from a cross pass by Madden.

And so Celts won by 2–0 to put the seal on a great season by winning the three cups, a feat, as already stated, which had not hitherto been accomplished by any club.

Although Celtic and Rangers have contested many

finals, too many indeed to be intimately described, the
fact that this was their first in this competition entitles it
to special mention.

Celtic's great feat of winning the three trophies in the
previous season was responsible for the special interest
which was shown in the Glasgow Final of 1892–93. The
rivalry which was afterwards to become such an import-
tant factor in Scottish football had not so far manifested
itself.

There were several changes in both teams from those
which had appeared in the Charity Final of the previous
season: M'Callum and Brady had gone from Parkhead
and Donald Gow from Ibrox—new men being Drummond, Mitchell, Hugh M'Creadie, Barker, Towie and
Blessington.

Rangers had not forgotten their defeat in that game
and were determined to avenge it, not to mention their
desire to put this comparatively new club in its place.

The clubs were represented by the following elevens:

CELTIC: Cullen; Reynolds and Doyle; Maley, Kelly
and T. Dunbar; Towie, Blessington, Madden, M'Mahon
and Campbell.

RANGERS: Haddow; Hay and Drummond; Marshall,
A. M'Creadie and Mitchell; H. M'Creadie, Davie, Kerr,
M'Pherson and Barker.

Referee: Mr. Hay, Dumfries.

A lot of rain fell previous to and during the game,
which rendered the surface very slippery.

M'Pherson and Barker performed well at the start,
and Drummond impressed when he cleverly pulled up
Towie as the latter was making for goal.

Davie Mitchell was also prominent in his tussles with the right winger and after Doyle had crossed to beat M'Pherson Celts started a dangerous attack.

M'Mahon, with his head, failed by inches to convert a corner taken by his partner, and Haddow elicited cheers when he twice saved grandly from Madden—Rangers' defence being rather worried at this stage.

Play veered round in favour of Rangers, and Cullen was beaten at the half-hour following some rather hectic play, during which some hard knocks were exchanged.

The splendid defensive work of Doyle for Celtic and Drummond for Rangers elicited cheers on many occasions, while their powerful kicking was generally admired.

Although Celtic played lovely football at the beginning of the second half it was Rangers who scored, Kerr increasing their lead in eight minutes.

Their two-goals advantage flattered Rangers, for whom Haddow was in marvellous form, although quite apart from that Celtic were most unfortunate, experiencing very hard lines on many occasions.

But it was apparently Rangers day, as despite Celtic's constant pressure, M'Pherson stole away to register still another goal for the Ibrox team five minutes from the end, M'Mahon scoring Celts' solitary crumb of comfort in the last minute.

It was a tremendously hard and at times brilliant game, although Rangers were rather fortunate to win—this being their first success in the competition.

It was a coincidence that the finalists of the previous season, Queen's Park and Celtic, should again reach the last stage of the competition, and peculiarly enough, the weather was responsible once more for two meetings between the clubs.

In spite of the hard frost and the doubt which existed as to whether the tie would proceed there was a splendid turn-out, £935 being drawn at the gates and £300 at the stands.

On this occasion the Association were parties to an arrangement that a friendly should be played, although there was nothing in the play of either team to let the public into the secret, both being tremendously keen.

Celtic won by 1–0, and this only served to whet the appetites of the public when the teams lined up on 11th March as follows:

CELTIC: Cullen; Reynolds and Doyle; Maley, Kelly and T. Dunbar; Towie, Blessington, Madden, M'Mahon and Campbell.

QUEEN'S PARK: Baird; Sillars and Smellie; Gillespie, M'Farlane and Stewart; Gullilland, Waddell, Hamilton, Lambie and Sellar.

Referee: Mr. Harrison, Ayrshire.

It must be realized that the Amateurs at this period of their career were struggling very hard to regain their former supremacy in the game.

They had appeared in ten of the nineteen finals since the competition had been instituted, and only once had they finished on the losing side.

What added to the importance of the present event was the fact that Queen's Park's only final defeat had been inflicted in the previous campaign and by the same opponents.

Then, of course, Celtic, to put it very plainly, were

looked upon as interlopers and not too welcome at that, but although they were regarded with feelings amounting almost to hatred in many quarters, their success and unquestioned talent were responsible for an increasing respect for their prowess.

The game was responsible for some magnificent football, and if the result was hailed with great delight by the general public it can truly be said that the same public were forced to acknowledge that the coming of Celtic had given football a tremendous impetus.

Read what the *Glasgow Herald* of the following Monday said:

" Never in the history of the game has there been a more popular victory. The scene at the end was the most enthusiastic we can recall in any Scottish Final, and it is safe to say that in their long and brilliant career, Queen's Park never stood higher in public opinion than they do at the present time.

" Although we say so much in favour of the Queen's, it is not to be supposed for a moment that we are blind to the part played by Celtic in Saturday's match.

" We congratulate Queen's Park on their victory which was really deserved, as in one or two points they were superior to Celtic, to whom we also offer our praise for the splendid way in which they contested the game and the sporting manner in which they accepted defeat."

This was penned by one of the fairest of the critics of the day, but even he apparently failed to take note of the many injuries sustained by the Celtic players in this great struggle in which they were fighting against the odds from the moment they set foot on the pitch.

The reception afforded the Amateurs when they appeared supplied ample proof of this, but of course Celts were by this time well accustomed to be regarded as the " villains of the piece ".

Queen's, assisted by a strong wind, gave their opponents' defenders a gruelling time during the early stages of the game, but when Campbell and M'Mahon got going play became more even.

A goal scored by Sellar ten minutes after the start, however, inspired the Amateurs, and in one of their desperate assaults Reynolds was injured in contact with Hamilton, resuming later in obvious pain.

This was the precursor of a succession of fouls, which assisted Celtic in keeping play in their opponents' quarters; but in a Queen's sortie Cullen was badly injured.

Worse was to follow, however: Doyle conceded what was generally thought to be a corner kick, but to the general amazement the referee awarded Queen's a goal, despite the fact that the ball had gone outside the upright.

Protests were of no avail, and to make matters even still worse W. Maley had sustained a facial injury during the siege previous to the award, and was now forced to retire. He returned to assist his now crippled colleagues a few minutes before the interval, which found Queen's leading by 2–0.

The Amateurs' goal ran a succession of very narrow escapes at the beginning of the second half, but there were other occasions on which Celtic might easily, by better finishing, have wiped out the deficit and gone well ahead.

It has to be remembered, of course, that in addition to the rather crippled condition of several of their players, they were affected by tremendous anxiety, which to a certain extent excused their mistakes.

Their bad luck appeared to have come to an end when Blessington scored, following a corner kick; but Queen's were determined to maintain their advantage, and despite many vocal protests from the crowd, kicked out on every occasion.

As a last resort, Dan Doyle moved up into the attack, but Queen's defence held out to avenge their defeat of the previous season.

Having fallen to Queen's Park in the Scottish Final and Rangers in the Glasgow Final, Celtic were given the opportunity of avenging at least one of these defeats when they opposed the Ibrox team in the last stage of the Charity Cup and incidentally of repeating their victory in last season's final over the same club.

Peter Dowds had returned from the South where he had spent a short time with Aston Villa, and another Anglo-Scot, Joe Cassidy, who had played for Newton Heath before returning home, partnered Johnny Campbell on the left.

Here are the teams:

CELTIC: Cullen; Doyle and Dunbar; Curran, Kelly and Maley; Madden, Blessington, Dowds, Cassidy and Campbell.

RANGERS: Haddow; Gow and Drummond; Scott, A. M'Creadie and Mitchell; Davie, D. M'Pherson, Kerr, H. M'Creadie and J. M'Pherson.

It was very early evident that the long and strenuous

season had left its mark on both teams, as the players were obviously tired.

Play was keen, nevertheless, and it was well for Rangers that they possessed such a splendid pair of backs, as Gow and Drummond alone stood between them and an avalanche of goals.

Celtic's recast attack was playing splendid football, and it was no more than their due when Campbell opened the scoring, adding another five minutes later.

Rangers were overwhelmed and devoted their energies to try and keep down the score, but Celts were in the mood and would not be denied.

It was a hectic finish to that first half. Blessington increased the lead to three and Campbell and Dowds brought the total to five ere the interval whistle sounded.

Rangers found their opponents in a less serious mood in the second half, but not to the extent of permitting them to score. Celts were content to indulge in some fancy football and so played out time without adding to their total.

And so the Charity Cup remained in their possession, and for the second successive year it had been gained by defeating Rangers in the final, but retribution was to follow, as history will relate.

The season 1893–94 proved to be one of the most important milestones in the Celtic-Rangers rivalry. Hitherto the Ibrox club had found their Parkhead opponents much too strong for them, and frankly did not enjoy the experience.

They had certainly won the Glasgow Cup in 1892–93, and possibly were beginning to realize that so well was this victory received by a public which welcomed the defeat of Celtic, no matter by which club, they might as well take full advantage.

Rangers accordingly began to set their house in order for the struggle which was to become much greater than they then imagined, and catching Celts between times, so to speak, or, to use a more common phrase, in a period of transition, the season 1893–94 greatly favoured the Ibrox combine.

Perhaps Rangers were just a little jealous of Celtic, and in a way one can sympathize with them.

For twenty-one years they had been striving unsuccessfully to win the Scottish Cup, and during all those years had only twice reached the final stage, being beaten by Vale of Leven in 1876–77 and again in the following season, when after drawing with the same opponents they, for reasons of their own, refused to replay.

Celtic in their short life of six years were making their fourth appearance, and had already one success to boast of, so that it is easy to realize how keen were Rangers to have their name inscribed on the trophy as the result of the final of 1893–94.

Hampden Park was the venue, the date 17th February, 1894, and the conditions none too good owing to the wet weather which had preceded the event and continued throughout.

Queen's Park officials had done their best to make the footing as good as possible, having given it a pretty fair sprinkling of hayseed, which in those days was regarded as scientific treatment.

CELTIC: Cullen; Reynolds and Doyle; W. Maley, Kelly

and Curran; Blessington, Madden, Cassidy, M'Mahon
and Campbell.

RANGERS: Haddow; Smith and Drummond; Marshall,
A. M'Creadie and Mitchell; Steel, H. M'Creadie, Gray,
M'Pherson and Barker.

Referee: Mr. J. Marshall, 3rd Lanark.

Celts were well and truly beaten on this occasion, as
Rangers, starting very confidently, quickly adapted themselves to the conditions and often had the opposing backs
in a quandary.

It will be easily understood that the Celtic forwards,
clever though they often proved themselves to be, received curtailed service from a half-back line which
feared to venture very far from their own goal area.

Still, M'Mahon and his colleagues gave Haddow many
anxious moments, the goalkeeper, as was usual when
playing against Celtic, putting in some wonderful saving.

There was no scoring during the first half, Celtic im-
proving a bit towards the interval, but Rangers went
ahead ten minutes after the resumption.

A pass by Barker to H. M'Creadie gave them the lead,
and the scene which followed was almost indescribable,
so great was the joy of the Ibrox following—for the day.

A titanic struggle ensued, Celtic making desperate
efforts to wipe out the lead while Rangers strove even
harder than before in the hope of increasing their advantage.

They succeeded in another ten minutes, Barker beating
Cullen with a magnificent drive; M'Pherson added a
third, but Celtic, although no doubt they realized that
they were beaten, never gave in.

They forced a succession of corners, and from one of these W. Maley scored—this was fifteen minutes before the end.

Their success came too late, however, as although they now played some great football the Ibrox rear division was as firm as a rock, and so the Cup went to Rangers for the first time after striving for twenty-two years for its possession.

Although they had won the League Championship, Celtic did not enjoy the prospect of finishing the season cupless, especially after their record triple success in 1891–92, and so were determined to hold the last of the three trophies—the Charity.

That Queen's Park, their Scottish Cup conquerors in the previous season, were their opponents provided them with an additional incentive, while Queen's were equally keen to confirm that victory.

Both teams showed changes, M'Arthur, McEleny and Divers being promoted, the latter to fill the place of M'Mahon who was ill.

Queen's Park brought in two youngsters who were later to become famous—Bob M'Coll and Willie Lambie—the latter appearing at outside left as partner to his brother.

The teams were as follows:

CELTIC: M'Arthur; Reynolds and Doyle; Maley, Kelly and M'Eleny; Madden, Blessington, Cassidy, Divers and Campbell.

QUEEN'S PARK: Baird; Sillars and Smellie; Gillespie, Robertson and Stewart; Gullilland, Waddell, R. S. M'Coll, J. Lambie and W. Lambie.

The Lambies were very dangerous on the Amateurs'

left, assisted by a strong breeze, but very soon Divers and Campbell, who were also combining well, asserted themselves, Sillars experiencing great difficulty in beating them back.

Celts were also handicapped by a brilliant sun, which often blinded them, but Dan M'Arthur created confidence by saving splendidly from M'Coll.

The half-back play on both sides was magnificent, although Celts' middlemen displayed better attacking power, with the result that they were the more dangerous.

The standard of play was very high and the crowd greatly appreciated a magnificent exhibition of dribbling by Blessington, who was finally thwarted by Baird who saved his shot.

In their efforts to show something for their wind advantage, Queen's made desperate attempts to score as the interval approached, to find M'Arthur in brilliant form, defying every effort on their part.

Terrific shots by Campbell and Cassidy marked the resumption, but Queen's suddenly went ahead when, after J. Lambie had prepared the way, Gullilland dashed between Reynolds and Doyle to open the scoring.

Celts were not long in recovering from this shock. They went right through from the centre kick and Cassidy gathered Blessington's cross to equalize.

It was all Celtic now. Queen's defenders were put through the mill and conceded corner after corner in order to save their charge, being relieved only by occasional raids by their wingers Gullilland and W. Lambie.

The winning goal came along six minutes from the

end. Doyle, that master of the art of placing the ball, took a free kick which left Blessington nothing to do but score and Celts were on the lead at last.

During the few minutes which followed Baird was almost constantly in action, saving great shots from Campbell, Cassidy and Dowds.

Celts were happy they had won for the third successive year the Charity Cup and had beaten their greatest rivals of the period.

In the story of the Club's part in the creation of countless records it is impossible to pass over one particular match in which, so far as the writer is aware, the highest score for a Scottish League First Division game was recorded in defeating Dundee by 11–0.

To their credit be it said, Celtic teams throughout the years were never guilty of " rubbing it in ", and even on this occasion there were times when they actually refused to score.

The match with Dundee is of course referred to. It was a League game and was played at Parkhead 26th October, 1895.

Dundee, who had opened the season rather disappointingly, were by this time on the up-grade, and during the three previous weeks had returned splendid results, so good indeed that they travelled south fairly confident of success. They had some first-class players in their ranks while Celtic showed several changes from the previous season.

CELTIC: M'Arthur; Meechan and Doyle; W. Maley, Kelly and Battles; Madden, Blessington, Martin, M'Mahon and Ferguson.

DUNDEE: Barrett; Darroch and Burgess; Dundas, Longair and Ferrier; Thomson, Sawers, Vail, M'Donald and Keillor.

Referee: Mr. J. Baillie, St. Bernards.

There had been heavy snow during the night and the ground early showed signs of being very sticky.

Dundee went off with a bang and Keillor tested M'Arthur with a long shot.

Quickly settling down to a confident game, Celtic pressed and M'Mahon slipped while in the act of converting Madden's cross.

Success was only delayed, however. The forwards, moving in beautiful unison, bore down on Barrett and Blessington finished the movement by scoring.

Dundee were outplayed and the ball travelling from right to left, Ferguson scored the second, Blessington adding another, followed by one from M'Mahon before the half-hour.

Dundee were in the depths, and to make matters worse Longair injured himself and retired.

By the interval Celts had six goals to their credit, and when the teams reappeared it was seen that Dundee were two players short, Ferrier being absent in addition to Longair.

The second half was farcical. Celtic were obviously holding back, although Martin, the centre-forward who had joined them from Hibs and who previously had failed to reveal his true form, was keen to establish himself.

He scored twice in the first few minutes, adding other two shortly after, Battles counting before the final goal at eleven minutes.

Only Barrett, Sawers and Keillor made any show; as a matter of fact the Celtic total could have easily been doubled, so great was the difference between the teams on the day's play.

Dundee received a lesson in football, one which they didn't forget for many a long day, and no doubt the licking they sustained was responsible for many a rough journey Celtic experienced in the succeeding years when they visited the town of Jute.

Although Rangers were cutting a more prominent figure in football in the mid 'nineties, Queen's Park still retained the affections of the vast majority of the devotees of the game.

Celtic, holders of the Glasgow and Charity Cups in 1894–95, having defeated Rangers in both finals, qualified for the last stage of the former in the following season, and as the Amateurs were their opponents the clash was looked forward to with considerable anticipation in view of previous exhibitions, and the fact that Queen's had ousted them in the first round of the Scottish Cup.

Professionalism had now been legalized and the occasion was regarded as an Amateur v. Professional affair—a test match as it were. The match was played at Ibrox and the Rangers' officials had made elaborate preparations for a great attendance—fifty police and four mounted constables, we were informed, had been engaged to keep us all in order.

There was another reason for the interest taken in this match. As has been hinted on more than one occasion, the followers of the other clubs were not taking kindly to the success of Celtic, and this was shown in no uncertain manner on every possible occasion—so long as Celtic were beaten it didn't matter who might be their conquerors.

The atmosphere created by this hostility had, however, little effect on those valiant Celts, indeed they appeared to thrive on it—in the three games previous to the Glasgow Final they had scored 23 goals for the loss of 1.

As already stated, preparations were made for a great crowd: there were eighteen pay-boxes utilized. Queen's Park were given the use of the new dressing-rooms under the covered stand where their officials and friends were accommodated, while Celtic used the old pavilion.

The weather unfortunately broke down and the attendance, although disappointing, beat the previous record of £500, drawn when the same clubs met in 1889–90, by £64.

CELTIC: M'Arthur; Meechan and Doyle; W. Maley, Kelly and Battles; Madden, Blessington, Martin, M'Mahon and Ferguson.

QUEEN'S PARK: Anderson; Gillespie and Smith; Allison, M'Farlane and D. Stewart; Crookston, Waddell, M'Coll, Cameron and Lambie.

Referee: J. Baillie, St. Bernards.

Celts were quickly into their stride and forced four corners in succession, the last of these, beautifully placed by Ferguson, being converted by Martin.

With traditional pluck Queen's replied hotly. The game was fierce, every second brought another thrill, and when M'Coll beat M'Arthur to equalize the excitement was intense.

Queen's were now the aggressors and M'Arthur was kept busy, so keen was the onslaught. Three corners were conceded and cleared and then the Celtic goal-keeper was given a rest.

M'Mahon appeared to have scored only to see Anderson making a marvellous save. Big Jock Gillespie was a hero in Queen's defence at this stage.

Battles was injured and taken off and Queen's, taking advantage of their opponents' handicap, scored two goals in the last five minutes of the first half through Crookston and Waddell.

A 3–1 lead at the interval rather flattered the Amateurs, who, but for some marvellous goalkeeping by Kenny Anderson, must certainly have lost several.

The crowd, which numbered 24,000, was delirious with joy at the prospect of a Celtic defeat, not knowing what the second half was to bring forth.

Many invaded the pitch at the beginning of the second portion, but in an orderly enough manner, and the police were not long in returning them to the terracing.

The restart was hectic. Celtic set about their apparently hopeless task with grim determination, disregarding the cheers which greeted every kick of their opponents.

Ferguson reduced the leeway and, a goal in arrears, the Parkhead fellows went all out for the equalizer.

The game was changed entirely, Queen's being forced to defend constantly, with Anderson performing miracles in goal.

The equalizer came at last and with twelve minutes to go Ferguson put Celtic on the lead. Two more followed the last on the call of time.

The excitement appears to have penetrated the Press Box, as the *Evening Times* representative, who was writing the game from the Celtic point of view—it was customary in those days to have each side's opinion reported—burst into " poetry " thus:

" Hurrah! At last the whistle sounds the call.
    Alas! Alas! Q.P. the jig is up
  Six goals to three. You must feel rather small,
    Brave, Bold Celts. You've nobly won the cup."

With success in the championship assured there remained the Charity Cup to be won, and with the prospect of establishing still another record it will be realized how keen were the Celtic players to win the trophy.

Renton had created a record by winning the Charity Cup four years in succession, 1886 to 1889, and Celtic had equalled that feat by winning it from 1892 to 1895.

Once again in the final, the incentive was great—no club had previously won the trophy more than four times in successive years—would they be the first to boast of five years' custodianship?

As fate would have it Queen's Park were again their opponents—they had disposed of Rangers in the semifinal by 6–1.

But they had to give of their best to defeat the Amateurs, and if they merited their 2–1 victory there was little more than their narrow margin in the game.

The Club's record at the end of 1895–96, eight years after their birth, was a formidable one. League Championship, three times; Scottish Cup, once; Glasgow Cup, four times; Glasgow Charity Cup, five times.

The next few years witnessed many changes in the Club's affairs. The old order was departed from with the formation of a limited liability company, and the personnel of the team almost entirely altered.

The season 1896–97, as it turned out, was the first since 1890–91 in which Celtic failed to win a single major honour.

Owing to some very questionable decisions on the part of the referee they were forced to replay the Glasgow Cup Final with Rangers, one of the latter's forwards actually sitting on M'Arthur's chest, what time a colleague was " scoring " the equalizer.

In the replay M'Mahon broke down, and without this great player's assistance for over half an hour Celts had to admit defeat by 1–0.

A week later there occurred the strike described else-where, which completely disorganized the team, as it deprived them of the services of three of their regular members.

Celtic's cup of sorrow overflowed, however, when in the first round of the Scottish Cup they went to Barr-head and were beaten by Arthurlie by 4 goals to 2.

It is no exaggeration to say that this was probably the greatest sensation ever known in Scottish football.

The section of the press which had contributed to dis-organization of the team owing to the strike was jubilant, but the more dignified organs were really sympathetic, knowing all the circumstances.

For reasons best known to themselves, Doyle and Gilhooley—the latter was the regular winger by this time—failed to appear. Madden, Dunbar, M'Mahon and Orr were nursing injuries and Russell had eye trouble—even M'Arthur was suffering from a head injury.

The " strikers " of course were not to be thought of, and these facts certainly warranted the statement in the *Glasgow Herald* on the following Monday which read:

" The Celtic Committee are certainly to be sympathized with for what with accidents, illness and suspensions of players, they found themselves utterly unable to get a decent team together, and from various causes over which they had no control only four of their regular players were available."

These four were Kelly, A. King, Blessington and Ferguson, and the team was made up as follows:

CELTIC: Cullen; J. King and Crossan; Farrell, Kelly and A. King; Morrison, Blessington, M'Ilvenny, Henderson and Ferguson.

ARTHURLIE: Airston; Smith and Hirst; Millar, Tennant and Boyd; Hannigan, Tait, Ovens, Spiers and M'Gregor.

Referee: D. M'Vicar, Greenock.

Although there was little or no understanding in the attack, there were opportunities enough to have established a lead early in the game, despite the brilliant saving of Airston, who kept goal for Arthurlie and was in the veteran stage.

But the Celtic backs, one of whom was a half-back and the other a left winger, were very weak and Hannigan scored for Arthurlie in twelve minutes. McIlvenny equalized eight minutes later, and although Celtic pressed incessantly they were unable to pierce the home defence.

Shortly before the interval Hannigan broke away and

crossed for M'Gregor to put the finishing touch on the ball to give Arthurlie a lead of 2–1 at the interval.

The Dunterlie Park of those days was by no means level or anything like it, indeed it was commonly known as the " Humph ", and playing down the hill in the second half the Barrhead men enthusiastically set about their task of making history.

How well they succeeded may be realized that the date and result of this tie has been asked and answered in the " Answers to Correspondents " column of the press some thousands of times since the event.

Cullen had a thankless task. His backs afforded him no protection from the vigorous thrusts of the local players, whom he had to face almost single-handed—he was certainly not to blame for the defeat.

Hannigan scored a third goal and M'Gregor a fourth; by this time the Celtic team had practically collapsed, only Cullen, A. King and Kelly offering any opposition to the jubilant locals.

Near the end Airston was again beaten, this time by Ferguson, but he had no occasion to worry as he had played a leading part in his club's victory by saving his charge in masterly fashion early in the game when Celts were doing fairly well.

This was the beginning of a series of defeats, as with so many men on the injured list new players were required but could not be had, and so for the first time in seven years, as already stated, they found themselves at the end of the season without a single honour.

Anno Domini was beginning to affect quite a number of the men who had given Celtic splendid service, and

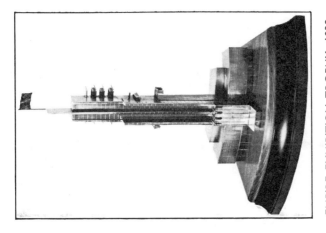

EMPIRE EXHIBITION TROPHY, 1938

EXHIBITION CUP OF 1901

1933

Top row: W. Maley, Manager; A. Thomson, R. Hogg, J. Kennaway, C. Napier, J. McGrory, W. McGonagle, and J. Quaskey, Trainer

2nd row: R. Thomson, C. Geatons, J. McStay, P. Wilson, and Hugh O'Donnell

Scottish Cup in centre

J. DELANEY

W. LYON

JOHN CRUM

1937

Top row: C. Geatons, R. Hogg, J. Kennaway, J. Morrison, W. Buchan, and George Paterson

2nd row: J. McMenemy, Trainer; J. Delaney, J. McGrory, W. Lyon, J. Crum, F. Murphy, and Manager W. Maley

JOHN THOMSON

1937-38

LEAGUE CHAMPIONS

Back row: C. Geatons, R. Hogg, J. Morrison, J. Kennaway,
G. Paterson, J. Carruth, and J. Divers
Front row: W. Maley, Manager; J. Delaney, M. McDonald, W. Lyon,
J. Crum, F. Murphy, and J. McMenemy (Trainer)

W. GROVES

DAN DOYLE

A. McMAHON

LEAGUE SHIELD

CELTIC STAND AND OFFICES FROM LONDON ROAD
ENTRANCE

PRESENTATION OF GLASGOW CHARITY CUP AT CITY CHAMBERS
JUNE, 1938

Sir John T. Cargill in foreground with Chairman Tom White
and W. Lyon holding Cup

On Board Anchor Liner S.S. "Caledonia"

A happy party taken at Detroit

AMERICAN TOUR, 1931

while the team of 1897–98 included veterans there were also several new faces.

Welford and Jack Reynolds, neither of them youngsters, had come up from Aston Villa with Johnny Campbell, who rejoined his first love, and Hugh Goldie and George Allan came from Everton and Liverpool respectively to Celtic Park along with Willie Orr from Preston North End.

The reconstructed team which included these players made a poor show in the Charity Cup at the end of the previous season, but hopes were entertained that with a summer's rest they would come into their own.

They started the season promisingly, and the expectations of their sponsors were justified when on the Autumn Holiday at Ibrox in a League match before 30,000 spectators they defeated Rangers by 4–0.

The teams on that occasion are worth giving, particularly as R. C. Hamilton was making his entry into " Old Firm " battles.

CELTIC: McArthur; Welford and Doyle; Goldie, Russell and Orr; Gilhooley, Campbell, Allan, McMahon and King.

RANGERS: Dickie; Smith and Drummond; Gibson, McCreadie, Glen; Low, Miller, Hamilton, Hyslop and Smith.

When the clubs met later in the season in the Glasgow Cup semi-final at Parkhead, Celts were naturally warm favourites at the beginning but very nearly came a nasty cropper.

McArthur sustained a serious head injury and Willie Orr was crippled, and to make matters worse, Rangers, taking full advantage, led by two goals to none.

E

Fortunately for Celtic, Gilhooley rose to the occasion and, gaining complete mastery over Jock Drummond, scored twice amid terrific excitement to force a replay.

At Ibrox a fortnight later both teams showed changes, Rangers being the more severely handicapped in this respect with Nick Smith, Miller and Hyslop absent.

Bobby Neil raised the Ibrox hopes by converting a penalty early in the game, and until Henderson equalized Celtic were rather disappointing.

A tremendous struggle ensued, Tommy Low on Rangers' right walking round King and Doyle like a master and Gilhooley fooling Drummond as he had done in the previous game.

The crosses, many of them most inviting, sent over by these lads were just as regularly refused, although in fairness to Celts it must be recorded that they were thrice thwarted by the uprights in the last ten minutes.

By a spin of a coin Rangers won the right to replay on Ibrox, and once more a great crowd was treated to a terrific battle; Hyslop scored for Rangers and Allan equalized for Celtic.

The last ten minutes saw Celts bombard Dickie's charge but all to no purpose, and there was nothing for it but to play an extra half-hour.

It was then that youth triumphed as R. C. Hamilton, young, lithe, virile, simply ran through his older opponents, Russell, Welford and Doyle, to score twice and enable Rangers to enter the final and beat Queen's Park by 4–0 to retain the cup.

The elusiveness of the national trophy during the years

which followed their success in 1892 was a source of worry
to the Celtic directors, who could not understand why
their teams, which could win four of the eight Championships as well as the Glasgow and Charity Cups with a
certain amount of regularity, and yet fail to win the
Scottish Cup.

When, therefore, they disposed of 6th G.R.V. by 8–1
and St. Bernards by 3–0 in the opening rounds and then
Queen's Park 2–1 and Port Glasgow 4–2, the latter being
in the semi-final, they found themselves in the final for
the first time since 1894—five years earlier.

That they were to be opposed by their great rivals
Rangers—who had beaten them on their last final
appearance and who had thrice won the cup, being
present holders—merely strengthened their determination
to have their name engraved on the trophy for the
second time.

As events proved they succeeded, and although their
margin of victory was not wide there was not the slightest
doubt regarding their superiority.

The game was summed up by the *Glasgow Herald*
in the following words, the writer's remarks regarding
the drawing power being particularly significant, when it
is recalled that they were written forty years ago:

" It was the best-behaved and most orderly concourse
of spectators of recent times. There were 25,000 and
even at that number there was not the slightest indication
of overcrowding at any part of the enclosure.

" When the increased rate of admission is considered
the attendance is a high testimonial to the drawing powers
of the clubs engaged.

" The weather was favourable but the football was disappointing, and all in favour of Celtic in the first half, the second portion being better but even then confined to one side.

" The feature of the game was the grand play of the Celtic half-backs and the utter incapacity of the Rangers' forwards.

" Celtic played the close-passing game in the first half, but opened up after the interval and fairly demoralized the Rangers' defence.

" Welford was the best back on view, giving one of the finest exhibitions seen in Scotland for many a day.

" Rangers' forwards failed, their half-backs were overworked and their backs sorely tried."

It is unnecessary to add to the foregoing beyond stating that Bell was crippled and that the Celts won by 2–0, the goals being scored by McMahon and Hodge.

The teams were as follows:

CELTIC: McArthur; Welford and Storrier; Battles, Marshall and King; Hodge, Campbell, Divers, McMahon and Bell.

RANGERS: Dickie; Smith and Drummond; Gibson, Neil and Mitchell; Campbell, McPherson, Hamilton, Miller and Smith.

Referee: Tom Robertson.

The result—Celtic's second success in the national competition—was hailed with delight by the Club's followers all over the country, and their satisfaction was increased when the Charity Cup was regained by defeating Rangers again and by the same score—2–0.

Celtic's cup history during the next few seasons and

their performances generally were not in keeping with those of the first ten years of their existence.

At the same time the directors were not idle. As pointed out in another part of this story of the Club, a new policy had been embarked upon—that of rearing their own players in preference to gathering in men from all over the country and from England, many of whom had been in the game for a considerable time.

It was not to be expected that success would immediately follow, as it took several years to blend the youngsters satisfactorily, but it was at last accomplished as I will show in good time.

The inauguration of the new policy did not come until the new century had been entered, and meantime as cupholders Celtic for the second successive season reached the Scottish Final again in 1899–1900 after disposing of Rangers at Celtic Park in the semi-final by 4–0 after a 2–2 draw at Ibrox.

This was to prove to be Queen's Park's last appearance in the event; they have not succeeded since in reaching the final stage.

The Amateurs were beaten by 4–3, but even in defeat their representatives were by no means disgraced as they played throughout with traditional vigour and pluck.

The teams were as follows:

CELTIC: McArthur, Storrier and Battles; Russell, Marshall and Orr; Hodge, Campbell, Divers, McMahon and Bell.

QUEEN'S PARK: Gourley; D. Stewart and Swan; Irons, A. J. Christie and Templeton; W. G. Stewart, D. Wilson, McColl, Kennedy and Hay.

Referee: Mr. J. Walker, Kilmarnock.

The game was played at Ibrox on 16th April, 1900, before an attendance of 17,000, and the weather was bright and clear, the only drawback being a rather gusty wind.

Queen's, facing the breeze, surprised the onlookers with their strength and energy, which they maintained throughout the game surprisingly, and their prospects of success were increased when Christie scored early in the game with a long shot.

Celts' short-passing game was meeting with no success against Queen's restless and tireless half-backs, and they wisely altered their tactics to long swinging passes which had the effect of keeping play in their opponents' territory.

After a succession of corner kicks, during which Queen's goal ran many narrow escapes, McMahon equalized with a beautiful cross shot.

Gourley was performing creditably in the Amateurs' goal but was unable to prevent Divers from adding the second—McMahon had headed the ball to him and the centre, also with the head, sent it into the net.

Another goal followed before the interval to give Celts a lead of 3–1.

The second half was not long in progress when Divers brought the score to four in a quick dash and the cup was as good as won.

Queen's, however, had other ideas, and profiting by the persistence of the Celtic forwards for close play, they reduced the leeway through D. Stewart.

Still fighting desperately, Queen's attacked with great

pluck and Battles headed into his own goal to give them a third, but their success ended there and Celts ran out comfortable if narrow winners by 4–3 to celebrate their third Scottish Cup victory and equal Rangers' triple success.

After winning the Scottish Cup in 1899 and again in 1900 Celtic opened their cup campaign of 1900–01 in brilliant fashion by defeating Rangers in the first round by 1–0.

Kilmarnock by 6–0 were their next victims and the third round saw them defeat Dundee at Dens Park by 1–0.

In the semi-final, which was played at Parkhead, St. Mirren went down before the conquering Celts—again the score was 1–0, and so the final was reached without the loss of a goal.

Although their opponents—Hearts—undoubtedly possessed a splendid team, which included the powerful Charley Thomson at centre-forward—this was previous to his centre-half days—and that master craftsman Bobby Walker of happy memory, they were not expected to be able to stand up to the confident Celts.

Although it is easy to be wise after the event, it was generally agreed that the Parkhead directors erred in playing Davidson, who had been absent from the team owing to injury, as he very early in the game gave proof that he had not properly recovered.

Storrier, who had been deputizing most satisfactorily, would have made all the difference and would probably have saved the defeat.

Quinn was another change; he displaced Findlay at

outside left, but no fault could be found with his inclusion as he did very well indeed, considering his inexperience.

The teams were as follows:

CELTIC: McArthur; Davidson and Battles; Russell, Loney and Orr; McOustra, Divers, Campbell, McMahon and Quinn.

HEARTS: Philip; Allan and Baird; Key, Buick and Hogg; Porteous, Walker, Thomson, Houston and Bell.

Referee: A. A. Jackson.

Although Celtic had the benefit of the wind in the first half Walker very soon put Hearts on the lead.

The ground was very heavy but despite this play was very accurate, and it was quite in keeping with the trend of the game that McOustra should head through from a well-placed free kick by Battles.

It appeared as if Celtic were going to take command, when in a helter-skelter rush McArthur was forced to punch the ball out and Bell meeting it returned it into the net to give the " Maroons " a 2–1 lead at the interval.

Celtic's prospects were the reverse of bright when a magnificent effort by Bobby Walker gave Thomson Hearts' third goal, but they fought like heroes and McOustra reduced the leeway.

A tremendous struggle now ensued, Hearts striving might and main to hang on to their slender lead and Celts straining every nerve to draw level.

Their pressure was bound to bear fruit, and reward came when McMahon equalized ten minutes before the end.

A draw was the worst that Celts could expect now,

indeed victory seemed to be theirs for the taking when one of these unaccountable accidents gave Hearts victory —and the cup.

To Walker, who throughout had been the master in the Hearts' attack, must be given the credit, although he was not the actual scorer.

Bobby had worked his way through and shot, but in going for the ball McArthur slipped and merely pushed it out. Bell was not far off, and grasping his opportunity, the left winger rushed in and smashed it past the prostrate goalkeeper.

Thus the *Glasgow Herald* comment:

" It was one of the greatest contests in the history of the game," wrote an experienced critic.

" Celtic played too close, for one thing, but Hearts owed their victory to the uncontrollable eagerness of their front line, the craft of Walker, and the cool resourcefulness of Allan, Baird, Hogg and Buick."

The defeat was a blow to Celtic, because they had set their minds on equalling Queen's Park's double record of winning the cup in three successive years, but they were doomed to further disappointments.

In the following season they had another good run in the cup, avenging Hearts' victory of the previous year by beating them at Parkhead by 2–1 after a draw at Tynecastle in the third round.

Once again St. Mirren fell to them in the semi-final— this time, however, at Paisley—and still again they met an Edinburgh club in the final—Hibernians.

Before proceeding to describe our second successive defeat in the final by an Edinburgh club, it may be

E 2

interesting to refer to the unsatisfactory ending to the Glasgow Cup competition only a few weeks earlier.

The rivalry between Celtic and Rangers had increased tremendously owing to the efforts of these clubs to build teams capable of ranking as the finest in the land.

Celtic had a slight lead in League Championships and several more Charity Cup successes—they were level in Scottish Cup victories, while Rangers had a slight lead in the City cup competition.

Consequently when they met in the Glasgow Cup Final of 1902 at Ibrox, the excitement was intense, and the game held the attention of the forty thousand spectators right up to the final whistle.

When the game ended the scores were level, each having scored once, and Celtic quite naturally anticipated that on their own ground they would improve on the result.

But there were difficulties to be overcome; they had not reached the stage when they could expect justice in the council chamber, and they were evidently prepared for trouble when the Glasgow F.A. committee met to make arrangements for the replay.

Rangers claimed that as the Association had selected Ibrox as the venue for the final, the game ought to be finished on that ground.

Celtic argued that it was only fair that the game should go to Parkhead, as Ibrox was the ground of one of the contesting teams, and to return there was to give Rangers an advantage. In addition, it was pointed out that Rangers' members tickets had been available for the first game—a privilege denied Celtic's members—and to repeat this would be grossly unfair.

The question was put to the council and Ibrox won by one vote!

Thereupon Mr. John O'Hara, the Celtic representative, handed in an official letter stating that in view of this decision his club scratched to Rangers!

Consternation reigned and the directors of both clubs, who were in waiting, were asked to try and come to some arrangement, but both were adamant—Celtic refusing to play unless at Parkhead, while Rangers sheltered themselves behind the Association's decision, and arrangements were made to present the cup and medals to Rangers in due course.

This incident, as can well be imagined, did not tend to lessen the rivalry nor the ill-feeling which now existed between the two clubs, but only a few weeks later something else occurred which swept away all rancour, and revealed what was best and sporting in the councils of both camps—I refer to the Ibrox disaster, which was followed by a great and widespread effort in which practically all Scottish and many English clubs participated in order to meet the many demands on Rangers and the S.F.A.

To take events in their order, however, the final of the Scottish Cup between Celtic and Hibernian should have been played on the Saturday following the International with England, but owing to the catastrophe which occurred on that occasion the game was put back a week, and on 24th April, 1902, the clubs met at Parkhead.

The gate was naturally affected, only £700 being drawn for admission. A further £120 was drawn at the stand, and this was handed over to the Disaster Fund.

Campbell was unfit and his absence caused a re-arrangement of the Celtic attack, McCafferty being brought in at outside right.

CELTIC: McFarlane; Watson and Battles; Loney, Marshall and Orr; McCafferty, McDermott, McMahon, Livingstone and Quinn.

HIBERNIANS: Rennie; Gray and Glen; Breslin, Harrower and Robertson; McColl, McGeachan, Divers, Callaghan and Atherton.

Referee: R. T. Murray, Stenhousemuir.

Divers, the ex-Celt, was very prominent in the early movements, having a steadying effect on his colleagues, although the wind was proving difficult.

Celts were showing good football but their shooting was atrocious, and as the game proceeded it was obvious that McMahon was most uncomfortable at centre.

Only Livingstone caused any trouble to Rennie in the first half, during which Hibs were surprisingly methodical and more than held their own, without, however, managing to score.

Early in the second half it appeared as if Celtic were going to win. Livingstone released a ball that seemed certain to beat Rennie, but it struck a colleague and was diverted on to the upright to be cleared.

Fifteen minutes from the end Hibs made a desperate effort. They forced a corner, and Bobby Atherton, whether by accident or design, sent it along the ground, McGeachan, very cleverly be it said, backheeling it into McFarlane's net.

This roused Celts and until the end they hammered at

Rennie's charge, even Battles being up among the forwards in order to force the equalizer.

It was all in vain, however; Hibernians won the cup
for the second time in their history and for the second
successive year the trophy went to the Capital, where, it
might be added, it has only once reposed since.

The appalling disaster at Ibrox Park on the occasion of
the Scotland v. England match of 1902 almost brought
financial ruin to Rangers as well as the S.F.A.

With praiseworthy promptitude, however, the Scottish
clubs as well as many from across the border offered
assistance in various forms, and among the schemes for
raising money was a tournament in which Rangers and
Celtic were opposed by Everton and Sunderland respectively.

In order to make these matches worth winning Rangers
put up the magnificent trophy which they had won in
the 1901 Glasgow Exhibition Football Tournament, and
the greatest interest was manifested in the competition.

Rangers defeated Everton and Celtic dismissed Sunderland, so that the great rivals were called upon to meet
once more, but on this occasion for a prize which would
be held by the winners as their own property—a unique
situation.

The final took place at Cathkin Park, and was regarded
as a game for the British Championship.

For an evening match, and played outwith the season—
the date was 17th June, 1902—the attendance of 7000
was regarded as very satisfactory, and right well were
the spectators repaid, as a brilliant exhibition of football
was served up.

The teams on that memorable occasion were as follows:

CELTIC: McFarlane; Watson and Battles; Loney, Marshall and Orr; Crawford, Campbell, Quinn, McDermott and Hamilton.

RANGERS: Dickie; Smith and Crawford; Gibson, Stark and Robertson; Lennie, Walker, Hamilton, Speedie and Smith.

Referee: J. Hay, Greenock.

Celtic immediately jumped into their stride, their right wing being in their most aggressive mood, Crawford's speed and Campbell's craft causing Rangers' defenders endless worry.

After a prolonged siege Quinn scored for Celtic.

Shortly after Campbell sent in a terrific shot which rebounded from the crossbar and Quinn, always ready to take a chance, promptly returned it into the net.

Rangers made herculean efforts to wipe out the deficit. The pace was hectic and the football of an exceptionally high standard.

Ten minutes before the interval McFarlane exhibited carelessness in dealing with a shot from Lennie by losing possession and Hamilton walked it into the empty goal.

Encouraged by this rather unexpected success Rangers threw everything into attack, and Speedie equalized three minutes later.

The second half was a scorcher, the ball travelling from end to end with tremendous speed as the wingers raided incessantly.

Both defences stood firm, however, the back play was magnificent, and by the end of the game the teams were still level.

Two evenings later they met again, and this game was simply a repetition of the first.

Space does not permit of details being given beyond the fact that at the end of ninety minutes each had scored twice.

An extra half-hour was entered into, and it appeared as if no decision would be arrived at when in the last half-minute Celtic scored to win the tournament and the Glasgow Exhibition Trophy.

Two months later another competition was staged in aid of the Disaster Fund for medals presented by Bovril, Ltd., for which Celtic and Rangers met at Hampden.

Both teams showed changes, McPherson appearing in goal for Celtic, McLeod at left back and Moir at right half.

For Rangers Drummond partnered Crawford, Graham appeared at outside right and Lennie moved over to support Alec Smith on the left, Bobby Neil displacing Jimmy Stark as pivot.

CELTIC: McPherson; Watson and McLeod; Moir, Loney and Orr; Crawford, Campbell, Quinn, McDermott and Hamilton.

RANGERS: Dickie; Crawford and Drummond; Gibson, Neil and Robertson; Graham, Walker, Hamilton, Lennie and Smith.

Rangers were quickly off their mark and Hamilton scored after the ball had been bobbing up and down in front of McPherson for some time.

Celtic were quite unperturbed by this blow. Indeed it merely seemed to make them realize that a reply was called for.

And what a reply! During the next ten minutes they beat Dickie four times. The Rangers' defenders were unable to stop the avalanche as first Hamilton, then Quinn and Campbell smashed balls past Dickie, a fourth being scrambled through in a mêlée.

It was a new experience for the Ibrox players, but they fought back magnificently to find Watson and M'Leod in their most determined mood and crossed over with the score standing, Celtic 4, Rangers 1.

Consternation was written all over their faces when Quinn added the fifth shortly after the resumption. In fairness to Rangers, however, it must be recorded that they never gave in and they were by no means flattered when Walker scored for them.

But that was their last crumb of comfort and with Quinn and Campbell adding to the score Celts scored a magnificent victory of 7-2 to secure the medals.

The following season saw Celtic and St. Mirren fight a prolonged battle in the first round of the national competition. They drew 0-0 at Celtic Park and at Paisley the replay ended 1-1.

Then to Ibrox, where with Celtic leading by 1-0 the game was stopped midway through the second half owing to a storm of wind and rain.

Back to Ibrox, Celtic won entry to the next round by 4-0 to dispose of Port Glasgow and then fall to Rangers by 3-0 at Parkhead.

In the following season they were to experience another long-drawn-out tie, but first they beat St. Bernards by 4-0 at Parkhead.

At Celtic Park in the second round they drew 1-1 with

Dundee, no goals being scored in the replay at Dens Park, but when the third game took place at Parkhead Celtic won by 5–0.

Third Lanark were disposed of in the semi-final by 2–1 and once again the great rivals were fated to meet in the final.

The game created tremendous interest, and was of course played on New Hampden. It was estimated that 65,000 witnessed this final.

Curiously enough, both teams were without their regular centre-forwards, Hamilton being missing from Rangers and Bennett from Celtic.

It is pleasing to relate that although on many occasions during the game excitement rose to fever heat the vast crowd was most orderly, and it is equally satisfactory to state that the players gave them no cause to behave otherwise.

The teams were as follows:

CELTIC: Adams; M'Leod and Orr; Young, Loney and Hay; Muir, M'Menemy, Quinn, Somers and Hamilton.

RANGERS: Dickie; Smith and Drummond; Henderson, Stark and Robertson; Walker, Speedie, Mackie, Donnachie and Smith.

Referee: Tom Robertson.

Celtic started with tremendous dash against a strong wind, and looked as if they were going to sweep all before them.

For a quarter of an hour they simply besieged Rangers' goal, but they failed to get through and the game assumed a new aspect.

Rangers suddenly wakened up and Speedie scored twice

in as many minutes, to the amazement of everyone, Celtic's players and spectators alike—probably Rangers themselves.

Celtic, however, soon recovered their balance, and playing with tremendous enthusiasm, drove Rangers into defence once more.

Sensationally Quinn broke through twice to score on each occasion, and the teams were level when they retired at the interval.

There was no holding Celts after the resumption. Quinn gave them the lead with an inspiring run and shot and until the end Rangers were forced to play second fiddle.

The *Glasgow Herald* summed up as follows:

" None but the most partial club follower can deny the superiority of Celtic as a team. They worked from the first kick of the ball to the close with a determination and purpose, a vigour and a combination which well merited victory, and that they only won by a single goal was due as much to their bad luck in front of goal as to their over-anxiety in the opening quarter of an hour.

" With a half-back line all triers and with a proper conception of the inside game they upset all the finessing tactics of Rangers' middle line, and although repeatedly checked by Smith and Drummond at the beginning they finally wore them out and forced their way to the front.

" Quinn was superb. He did not worry any in helping Loney but kept lying well up between Rangers' backs, waiting for a rush such as R. C. Hamilton enjoys and puts to use, and this proved the most profitable game in the end.

" Rangers' defence failed to stay the full time and to

this more than perhaps anything else must be attributed their downfall.

" Celts were the younger and also the fresher team, and the lesson will doubtless be taken to heart at Ibrox.

" Celtic had some misgivings at having to drop Bennett for Quinn, but the result must have removed all these by this time, for the centre-forward not only played quite up to anything that Bennett has yet shown but scored three goals for his club, a record which will be hard to beat."

The team was now a splendid blend of youth and experience, and the management looked with considerable confidence to the future.

Their confidence was thoroughly rewarded, as in 1904–5 a run of success was entered upon during which the League Championship was won eleven times in fifteen years.

During the period preceding the War, starting from 1904–5, they won the Scottish Cup five times, the Glasgow Cup seven times, and the Charity Cup nine times.

For the first and only time in the history of the League they held the Championship on six successive seasons, a feat which was recognized by that body who presented them with a shield to mark the occasion.

Their previous record of five successive victories in the Charity Cup competition they excelled, as from 1912 to 1918 inclusive they won the trophy and in 1907–8 they won everything—Championship, Scottish Cup, Glasgow Cup and Charity Cup—a performance hitherto un-equalled.

To describe even a small proportion of the many brilliant performances which assisted in the creation of these records would occupy far too much space and might even become monotonous, but I feel that the final of the Scottish Cup of 1908–9 cannot be passed over as it led to an exhibition of mob law which fortunately for the good name of football had never happened before, nor has it been repeated.

Unfortunately Celtic and Rangers were the unfortunate and perfectly innocent actors in the tragedy which had such a disastrous ending, and the circumstances to which the trouble was attributed were as follows:

We had drawn at our first meeting and at the end of the replayed final we were again level.

The rule at the time made no provision for extra time in the event of a second draw, but unfortunately, due, it was believed, to a mistake on the part of a pressman, his paper stated that an extra half-hour would be played, and evidently this was believed by a section of the crowd.

At all events when the final whistle sounded and the players retired from the field an unruly mob invaded the field and proceeded to destroy everything they could lay their hands upon.

Not content with this, some of them set fire to the pay-boxes and the entrances were destroyed, in short, a most disgraceful riot ensued.

No blame was attached to either club, indeed one of the foremost writers on the game said:

" The Ibrox disaster was a calamity, this outbreak was a disgrace; there was never less occasion for disturbance. The game was fairly fought and ended as most of the play indicated, indeed the majority of the spectators while regretting the circumstances had resigned themselves to seeing the replay when the hooligan element broke loose.

" There was a false impression that the tie would be played to a finish, but had the public known the rules there would have been no demand for extra time and no waiting for the reappearance of the players.

" There is no suspicion of arrangement—those who know the intense feeling which exists between the clubs regard such a thing as absurd.

" Celtic are in a desperate position so far as fixtures are concerned, and by this time are thoroughly tired mentally and physically."

That was perfectly true, as our League fixtures had got in arrears owing to three matches in the Glasgow Final with Third Lanark, a replay in the semi-final of the Scottish with Clyde and the two finals with Rangers.

The S.F.A. held a special meeting to consider the position and decided to withdraw the cup for the season—a conclusion which no reasonable person nor the clubs concerned for that matter made any objection to.

The first of the two games was played before a record crowd of 70,000, the teams being:

CELTIC: Adams; M'Nair and Weir; Young, Dodds and Hay; Munro, M'Menemy, Quinn, Somers and Hamilton.

RANGERS: Rennie; Law and Craig; May, Stark and Galt; Bennett, Gilchrist, Campbell, M'Pherson and Smith.

Referee: J. B. Stark, Airdrie.

Play started very briskly, both goals being tested during the first few minutes.

Quinn, who was regarded as the danger point, opened the scoring. He followed up a long clearance to beat both Rangers' backs and head past Rennie.

Rangers fought back with great vigour, M'Pherson being particularly dangerous, but the Celtic halves were in splendid form.

After the interval Bennett and Campbell changed positions and Rangers' attack improved tremendously, so much indeed that eighteen minutes from the end Gilchrist equalized and three minutes later Bennett put them on the lead.

A desperate struggle ensued and close on time Munro flashed in a shot which Rennie clutched all right but in evading Quinn he swung the ball over the line and the referee, who was well placed, had no hesitation in awarding a goal, the game ending 2–2.

There were 60,000 present at the replay on the following Saturday. Celtic substituted Kivlichan for Munro at outside right and Rangers made three changes, Gordon displacing May, and Campbell and Gilchrist dropping out in favour of M'Donald and Reid—the attack being Bennett, M'Donald, Reid, M'Pherson and Smith.

This time Rangers were the first to score, Gordon beating Adams after twenty minutes' play. The players didn't spare themselves and " Sunny Jim " was forced to retire to have his head stitched as the result of a collision with Galt.

Celts were playing great football but couldn't score, although with the exception of the last ten minutes of the first half they were easily the better side.

Rangers impressed for a few minutes following the resumption and then Celts regained the mastery. To score was, however, a different matter as Rangers, determined to hang on to their lead, concentrated on defence.

At last Quinn equalized, but that was the end of the scoring, and so ended the most unsatisfactory competition in the history of the Scottish Cup.

Our successful League run came to an end at the close of the 1910–11 season—we had our share of the other honours—but we won the Scottish, beating Hamilton Accies in the final, and again in 1911–12 by beating Clyde, also starting our long run of seven successive Charity Cup victories.

In 1913–14 we were given the opportunity of avenging our Scottish Cup Final defeat of 1902 as we met Hibernians in the final.

Ibrox Park was the venue and there were 56,000 present in the expectation of seeing a keen game.

Our luck was out that season so far as home draws were concerned as not once were we fortunate in the ballot, our opponents having choice of ground in every round.

It is true we beat Clyde in the first round at Parkhead but that was after we had drawn 0–0 at Shawfield—we entered the second round by a 2–0 victory.

Then to Forfar where we won 5–0, on to Motherwell in the third round to win by 3–1, and in the semi-final we beat Third Lanark by 2–0.

Many changes had taken place in the team since the riot year; only M'Nair, Dodds, Young and M'Menemy of that lot took part in this final.

CELTIC: Shaw; M'Nair and Dodds; Young, Johnstone and M'Master; M'Atee, Gallagher, Owers, M'Menemy and Browning.

HIBERNIANS: Allan; Girdwood and Templeton; Kerr,

Paterson and Grosert; Wilson, Fleming, Henderson, Wood and Smith.

Referee: T. Dougary, Bellshill.

Quinn had more or less dropped out owing to knee trouble and M'Coll, who was regarded as his successor, although a newcomer, was also unavailable. Owers had been transferred from Clyde to help us out some time before but had not proved very satisfactory, although he still retained his place.

Hibs made a very plucky effort but were very much flattered with a draw at the end of the game as had Owers—to mention only one of the forwards—accepted half the gifts sent him, we would have won with something to spare.

In the replay he was dropped, M'Coll being pronounced fit to play, and as it turned out his inclusion made all the difference.

We were set to face a brilliant sun and Hibs took due advantage as they lashed the ball in the air and generally attempted to get our lads on the run.

They missed one great chance early in the game when three of their forwards failed to reach a pass, Charley Shaw being in the same category.

Then Celts' forwards got going; M'Atee sent over a lovely ball and M'Coll deftly diverted it past Rennie to open our account.

Three minutes later the clever young leader sent in a magnificent shot which Rennie could only palm out and M'Coll, who had stumbled after delivering his shot, struggled to his feet to return it into the net.

Five minutes from the interval Browning scored a

third and the cup was as good as won, but the scoring
was not yet finished as early in the second half M'Atee
sent across a ball from right to left for Browning to
register number four, Hibs taking a slight consolation
when Smith scored their solitary goal shortly after.

Strangely enough, our next appearance in the Scottish
Final was again in company with Hibernians—in 1922–
23, the War period having brought many changes as
time must do.

A new team had been gathered together and in the
process of discovering the proper blend we had not
figured very prominently in the post-War Scottish Cup
competition.

The Championship had certainly been won in the previous season, and while it was realized that the team
could be improved we took a certain amount of satisfaction from the winning of the 1921–22 Flag and another
final victory over Hibernians, whom we defeated by 1–0.

Our exit from the cup in the first round at the hands
of Kilmarnock was a distinct blow, of that there was no
doubt; indeed 1923–24 must be included in the category
of lean years, and there were several of them around
that period which for the Club was one of rebuilding.

Still, as always, Celtic was a force to be reckoned with,
and if Rangers were rapidly gaining on us in League
Championships, we were still well ahead in Scottish Cup
victories and further increased our lead in 1924–25, thus
beating Queen's Park's record of ten cup successes.

We had started off by beating Third Lanark at Cathkin
Park and in the next two rounds disposed of Alloa and
Solway Star respectively.

The fourth round was responsible for a rare old tussle with St. Mirren.   We drew at Paisley o–o and in the replay at Parkhead each scored one.

Ibrox Park was the venue selected by the S.F.A. for the third meeting, but it was only by a single goal—the only one scored in the tie—that we won through.

The semi-final saw us paired with our old rivals—Rangers—who had been struggling for years to win the cup and once more they were doomed to disappointment, as we defeated them by 5–o at Hampden.

Dundee were our opponents on this occasion—their second appearance in the final, their previous one being in 1910 when they defeated Clyde at the third time of asking.

Our indifferent performances in the League and Glasgow Cup competitions had been slightly atoned for by our semi-final victory, but on the whole Dundee were regarded as probably winners.

This no doubt accounted for the remarkable attendance, which numbered 75,157—which, although short of that of the Albion Rovers-Kilmarnock Final—the first after the War—it surpassed all others.

The line up was as follows:

CELTIC: Shevlin; W. M'Stay and Hilley; Wilson, J. M'Stay and Macfarlane; Connelly, Gallagher, M'Grory, Thomson and M'Lean.

DUNDEE: Britton; Brown and Thomson; Ross, W. Rankine and Irving; Duncan, M'Lean, Halliday, J. Rankine and Gilmour.

Referee: T. Dougary, Bellshill.

An ex-Celt figured prominently during the first half—

I refer to David M'Lean—as in addition to causing our defence quite a lot of trouble he scored in half an hour to give Dundee a 1–0 lead at the interval. The Dens Park half-backs were in splendid form, completely holding up our inside forwards, and from the ovation accorded the Dundee players as they retired at half-time it was evident they were regarded as ultimate winners.

Our forwards were a different lot in the second portion, however. They played magnificent football and but for some truly marvellous saving by Britton must certainly have gone well ahead.

This half was one long thrill, as the Dundee defenders were constantly under fire. For twenty minutes they held out, and when they were at last beaten it was by an effort which will never be forgotten by those who were privileged to be present.

" Patsy " Gallagher was the hero of the incident. He obtained possession of the ball and beat man after man by a twisting and turning movement which took him right in on goal, and he finished it by literally carrying the ball into the net.

Friend and foe cheered alike. It was one of these efforts which have to be seen to be appreciated, and it was with difficulty, so I was told after the game, that the Dundee players refrained from joining in the tribute to that wonderful little player.

The goal brought relief in more ways than one. The strain on the crowd had been terrific, it was painful, as one gentleman put it, during the long bombardment of the Dundee goal, which might have fallen a dozen of times.

The Dundee rear division continued to defend dog-gedly and it was not until four minutes from the end that M'Grory headed the winning goal following a free kick.

The next couple of seasons saw us reach the final to lose to St. Mirren in 1925–26 and to beat East Fife in 1926–27.

These experiences, admirable though they were—it is always good to reach the final—do not call for details—space does not permit the description of every game, but I feel that I would be lacking in my duty and unfair to a great club if I failed to mention specially Rangers' Cup victory in 1928–29.

To realize thoroughly the situation at that period it must be remembered that for twenty-five years Rangers, while they had won League Championships, Glasgow and Charity Cups galore, had failed to win the National Trophy.

Worse than that they had only twice appeared in the final, since 1908, to be beaten rather unexpectedly by Partick Thistle and Morton respectively, and it seemed as if Dame Fortune had a special grudge against them so far as the Scottish Cup was concerned.

There were many therefore, when we met at Hampden in the 1928 Final, who anticipated still another Rangers defeat, but fate, on this occasion, decreed otherwise, as they won, and won handsomely, by 4 goals to 0.

The crowd was a record one—note how Celtic have figured in all the records established in football—the attendance being 118,115, the official returns putting the drawings as £5755 9s. 6d., but the game was worthy of it.

Although the conditions were not conducive to an exhibition of really high-class football, the players mastered them to such an extent that a critic of knowledge and experience complimented them on " their all round decisiveness and intelligence, which made the contest one of the finest ever witnessed in a Scottish Final ".

It was truly a meeting of giants, a game in which tactics, strategy and craft were ever in evidence; and while Rangers eventually triumphed as they merited, they were indebted to many " breaks " which, I willingly agree, had been denied them during their quarter of a century's failure to win the National Trophy.

Let me give the names of the players who took part in this memorable game:

CELTIC: J. Thomson; W. M'Stay and Donoghue; Wilson, J. M'Stay and Macfarlane; Connolly, A. Thomson, M'Grory, M'Inally and M'Lean.

RANGERS: T. Hamilton; Gray and R. Hamilton; Buchanan, Meiklejohn and Craig; Archibald, Cunningham, Fleming, M'Phail and Morton.

Referee: W. Bell, Hamilton.

Rangers evidently had laid their plans carefully, as when they found themselves facing a strong wind on a hard, dry ground, they concentrated on defence to the extent of closely marking their opposing inside forwards, and leaving Archibald, Fleming and Morton to raid when opportunity offered.

Consequently the game was one of checkmate, but none the less enjoyable to witness—it was a real battle of wits.

I recall one glorious save by Tom Hamilton which, I

am convinced, turned the scale in Rangers' favour. I refer to the occasion on which A. Thomson's shot appeared certain to count, when the goalkeeper miraculously got to it.

This, and another after M'Inally, with a most subtle move, opened up the Rangers' defence and gave M'Lean a great opportunity, Hamilton again distinguishing himself, indicated that luck was not going to be with us on this occasion.

The second half saw Rangers at their very best—the whole team played with admirable precision and confidence.

In ten minutes they went ahead by means of a penalty kick about which there was no dubiety, W. M'Stay having punched out the ball as it was travelling into the net.

Celtic, realizing the possibility of defeat, played up gamely and continued to do so after M'Phail had added the second goal midway through the second half.

Archibald, who was in brilliant form and had, by this time, got the better of our makeshift left back, added two more, to give Rangers perhaps one of their greatest and certainly one of the most appreciated victories throughout their long history.

Two years later Rangers scooped the pool as we had done in 1907–8, but in 1930–31 we again won the cup after one of the most exciting finishes one could hope to see. I refer to the Final with Motherwell.

Here are the teams:

CELTIC: J. Thomson; Cook and M'Gonagle; Wilson, M'Stay and Geatons; R. Thomson, A. Thomson, M'Grory, Scarff and Napier.

MOTHERWELL: M'Clory; Johnman and Hunter; Wales, Craig and Telfer; Murdoch, M'Menemy, M'Fadyen, Stevenson and Ferrier.

Referee: P. Craigmyle, Aberdeen.

There was little to indicate during the game that there was to be a sensational finish to it, although there were occasions when our players, rightly or wrongly, believed that they had cause for complaint.

At all events, Motherwell seemed to be well on the way to winning the Cup on their first appearance in the Final, as with only eight minutes to play they led by 2–0.

They were at this stage concentrating on defence, and taking particular care of Napier, who was regarded by them as our most dangerous shot.

Altering his tactics for once, however, the winger elected to send over a high soft-looking lob, and M'Grory, ever ready to grasp an opportunity, laid it safely in the back of the net.

Even then Motherwell looked likely winners—surely Celtic couldn't score again in the last few minutes.

But score they did, and in such a sensational manner that I take the liberty of quoting the *Glasgow Herald* report of the incident. My own recollection, blurred by the tremendous excitement of the moment, is too vague to be depended upon. " The last minute of this game provided the incident which will be longest remembered by the 105,500 people who attended Hampden Park.

" The ball lay in the goal net, R. Thomson danced for joy, while the other Celtic players hugged each other with delight.

" Pandemonium prevailed on the terracing, Alan

Craig lay on the ground after heading the ball through his own goal, a picture of dejection.

" This is what led up to the sensation. R. Thomson gained possession, worked upfield, and as Hunter advanced to tackle him, doubled back to send over a harmless enough looking ball.

" Craig, evidently flustered and doubtful as to what he should do, rose to head clear, but failed to take the ball cleanly, and instead guided it past M'Clory."

Thus the game was saved for us. We had actually given up hope, but we were now perfectly confident as to the ultimate verdict, indeed I really believe we had Motherwell beaten before the game started.

I certainly sympathized with Motherwell, as fate had undoubtedly been most unkind. Too often in the past had I been disappointed although, I admit, never in such a sensational manner.

As I say, we were very confident, and felt even more so when R. Thomson scored in ten minutes, and we continued to hold the upper hand.

Motherwell, however, had got over their nervous period, and took heart when fifteen minutes later Murdoch equalized.

We were not long level, however, as four minutes later M'Grory restored our lead, and R. Thomson added the third to give us a 3–1 advantage at the interval.

Possibly Motherwell, recalling our late recovery on the previous Saturday, thought they might do likewise, and their hopes revived when Stevenson scored for them in twenty-five minutes.

Encouraged by this success they threw caution to the

winds, risking everything in the hope of snatching the equalizer, but all in vain; instead it was Celtic who scored in the closing minutes—Napier adding the fourth goal four minutes from the end.

Motherwell, I am glad to relate, achieved at least one of their great ambitions in the following season, when they won the League Championship, but when they met Celtic in the Final of the Scottish Cup in 1933, they fared no better than on their previous appearance in the event, as we again won—this time, however, by the narrow margin of 1–0.

The teams on this occasion showed changes. John Thomson had died in a tragic manner, and Peter Scarff was suffering from illness which brought about his demise seven months later, while Cook had been transferred to Everton—Kennaway, Hogg and H. O'Donnell being the newcomers.

Motherwell had two new backs, Crapnell and Ellis for Johnman and Hunter, and Blair replaced the unfortunate Craig, who went to Chelsea, while M'Kenzie appeared at left-half instead of Telfer, but the same attack was still functioning. Here are the teams:

CELTIC: Kennaway; Hogg and M'Gonagle; Wilson, M'Stay and Geatons; R. Thomson, A. Thomson, M'Grory, Napier and H. O'Donnell.

MOTHERWELL: M'Clory; Crapnell and Ellis; Wales, Blair and M'Kenzie; Murdoch, M'Menemy, M'Fadyen, Stevenson and Ferrier.

The game, witnessed by 102,339, was rather disappointing in play, never attaining the standard of the previous Final meeting of the clubs.

F

Motherwell impressed at the beginning, and Kennaway had some fine saves, but as the game wore on Celtic gradually took a grip which they never let go, and had they taken more risks might have won more easily.

The only goal came three minutes after the interval, the game being notable for the many miskicks and rebounds which deprived both sides of scoring chances.

I come now to the last of the milestones in the fifty years of the Club's history—the winning of the Scottish Cup for the fifteenth time, a game regarding which I do not think it is necessary to describe as the details must be fairly fresh in the memory of my readers.

Suffice to say that we defeated Aberdeen by 2–1—a victory which I think will be acknowledged was worthily earned; but this Final had another feature which is particularly interesting to those who have followed my poor efforts to tell the story of Celtic, as well as to those who for various reasons have a more intimate interest in the Club.

When I mention that the Final of 1936–37 was attended by the magnificent number of 144,303 spectators, I recall the struggles of our early days—days when nothing but great enthusiasm and dogged determination kept the flag flying.

While paying willing and due tribute to our opponents on the many occasions on which records were established, I maintain that the Celtic Club has made a tremendous contribution to the game in Scotland, and I claim that the position it occupies, quite apart from its many great achievements, entitles it to the respect, even admiration, of every true sportsman.

That this is seldom withheld I acknowledge, willingly, and with all the greater satisfaction when I recall the days when the Club was young, and regarded with feelings which would not be tolerated in this more enlightened and broadminded age.

I am conscious that there may have been many matches which I might have referred to, that time may be responsible for slight discrepancies in those I have described; but I have performed my task in good faith, and I trust with due regard to the feelings of all who may have recollections of them.

Some Famous Celts

Dan Doyle, born in Paisley, was acknowledged as one of the greatest of Scottish backs, and probably was the finest who ever served our Club. Of magnificent physique, he possessed such uncanny judgment that his lack of speed was never noticeable, and in the taking and placing of a free kick he stood alone. Before settling down at Celtic Park he served several clubs, including East Stirlingshire, Newcastle East End, Grimsby Town and Everton. During the ten seasons he spent with us before giving up the game, Doyle won all the possible honours and playing for Scotland put up some wonderful displays. Attacked by a malignant disease, he died at the age of 55 after a lingering illness. I was with him a few hours before the end, and he talked of many incidents of his career, being particularly proud that he had played his part in making Celtic history.

Played *v.* England, 1892, 4, 5, 7, 8; *v.* Wales, 1893; *v.* Ireland, 1895, 8; *v.* English League, 1892, 3, 4, 5, 6, 7, 8; *v.* Irish League, 1896, 9.

Peter Dowds, a Johnstone lad, was generally regarded as the greatest all-round player we had seen at Celtic Park; he could step into any position and fill it not only satisfactorily but with distinction. He was probably, however, seen at his best in the intermediate line, where his intuition made the robbing of opponents look simple. After a short spell with the Club he allowed himself to be persuaded to go South, where he assisted Aston Villa and Stoke, but returned to us in 1894. The old ability was still in evidence, but his health had suffered and lung trouble developing he died at an early age. Only one honour came his way, a cap against the Irish League in 1892.

The late **Mr. James Kelly** was a native of Renton and earned his great reputation as a player in the ranks of the famous team of that village of 1886–88, where he assisted them to win the World's Championship. For Celtic he played from 1888 until 1897, during which time he was one of the mainsprings of the Celts. Retiring from the field in 1897, he was at once made a Director and until his death in 1931 sat continuously on the Board of Management. His fame as a player needs no recounting as his name is known wherever the game is played. As a centre half-back he had few equals and no superior.

Of a kindly disposition, his work on the Club's Board of Management was great, and his memory will live long with those privileged to know him.

He won innumerable medals for Cup and League victories whilst his International caps were as per annexed list.

He played *v.* England, 1888, 9, 90, 92, 93; *v.* Ireland, 1886, 93, 96; *v.* Wales, 1894; *v.* English League, 1893, 4, 5, 6; *v.* Irish League, 1895, 6, 7.

May the turf he loved to tread in life rest kindly on him in his last sleep.

Sandy M'Mahon was one of the Club's earliest stars and certainly one of its brightest, and was regarded as the most marvellous header of the ball of the period.

Tall, almost ungainly in appearance, Sandy depended on footwork and the deceptive swerve to beat an opponent. Of speed he had little. His judgment of the flight of the ball when free or corner kicks were being taken was simply marvellous, and despite the fact that there were always several opponents set to watch him, at these times he scored a great number of goals with his head. Although he was regarded as a centre-forward during the very short time he spent with Hibernians before coming to Parkhead, it was as an inside left he made his reputation in partnership with Johnny Campbell, who in those days played on the wing.

After his best days as a player were over he spent a season with Partick Thistle.

Sandy was capped v. England in 1892, 3, and 4; v. Wales, 1902; v. Ireland, 1893, 1901; v. English League 1892, 3, 4, 5, 1900; v. Irish League, 1894, 6, 9; v. Canada, 1891.

He was born in Selkirk, and as a youth played a few games for Darlington St. Augustines.

James M'Menemy, a typical Celtic player, earned the cognomen " Napoleon " for the strategy with which his every move was imbued, and his wonderful positional sense. The football pitch to him was a chess-board; he was continually scheming and plotting and seldom if ever troubled himself with the physical side of the game—he had no need.

Playing for Rutherglen Glencairn he received many temptations to turn senior, but James had his ambition —to become a Celtic player—and it was gratified.

He was judiciously nursed in it and was worth it, as in due course he became one of the finest inside forwards of all time, although the brilliance of Bobby Walker kept him out of the International limelight for some years. When it was believed that his best days were over Jimmy was given a free transfer, and joining Partick Thistle he assisted them to a great extent in winning the Scottish Cup in 1921–22. He is again with us at Parkhead as trainer and coach.

Capped *v.* England, 1910, 11, 14; *v.* Wales, 1910, 11, 12, 14; *v.* Ireland, 1905, 9, 11, 14, 20; *v.* English League, 1908, 10, 11, 12, 13, 14, 15, 20; *v.* Irish League, 1910, 11, 15, 20; *v.* Southern League, 1915.

James Quinn is recognized as the greatest centre-forward we have ever possessed, and we have had many fine leaders. He was playing for Smithston Albion, whose ground was opposite the house in which he lived, adjacent to Croy Station, and working in the pits when we heard of him, and his position at the time was outside left. His pluck and physique led me to believe that something might be made of him, but it took me some time to persuade him that he could make good in 'senior football. Jimmy did not develop very quickly, being very shy, but his chance came and with it fame when he was included at centre-forward in the Scottish Cup Final of 1903–4 *v.* Rangers, in which he practically won the match for us, scoring our three goals.

A strong robust player possessed of a wonderful pair of shoulders which he used to great advantage and more fairly than he was given credit for.

Quinn was subjected to a lot of abuse in the course of his fourteen years' service. He seldom objected to anything done to himself, but deeply resented ill-treatment to any of his colleagues less able to stand up to it, and this brought trouble on his head which was often more harsh than circumstances demanded.

His caps were *v*. England, 1908, 9, 10, 12; *v*. Wales, 1906, 10, 12; *v*. Ireland, 1905, 6, 8, 10; *v*. English League, 1904, 5, 6, 9, 10, 12; *v*. Irish League, 1909, 10.

Peter Somers was as nimble of foot as he was nimble of tongue. He was a pastmaster in the art of repartee. When a youngster with Cadzow Oak, we went, on the advice of a friend, to watch Peter play. So well did he play that we were certain that he would make the Celtic grade. We signed him, but did not keep him at Celtic Park. We let him go " on loan " to Blackburn Rovers. He was a Rover for a season and a half. When we wanted him back, the Rovers pressed us to accept a big sum for his transfer. We refused, and Peter returned to Celtic a full-fledged and highly accomplished journeyman.

For Celtic he was a grand servant. Of all the men who have played the inside forward game for us the M'Menemy, Quinn, Somers combination was the best. Peter had no love for rough-and-tumble football. He was a subtle strategist. The way he evaded encounters with the opposition and got away with the ball was as entertaining as it was cute. His positional play was a

treat.   He ended his playing days with Hamilton
Academicals. Peter died a few years ago.

James Young (Sunny Jim).   Celtic have never
had a more whole-hearted player. He was a half-back
of the rugged type, but there was class in his ruggedness,
whilst for stamina he stood in the front rank.   His
enthusiasm inclined him sometimes to excesses, but a
kinder-hearted fellow never wore a Celtic jersey.

We got Young from Bristol Rovers, to which club
he had gone from his native Kilmarnock as a junior.
He was recommended to us as a player of exceptional
promise, and as he wanted to get back to Scotland we
fixed him on the recommendation of Bobby Muir.
Nor did we have cause to regret doing so. We tried
him out against Third Lanark, and he gave full satisfaction.   In time he became captain of Celtic, and a
splendid one he made. A player of dauntless courage,
he served Celtic faithfully and ably for many seasons.
His playing career ended prematurely. A damaged knee
brought it to a close, and not long after, while motor-
cycling with a friend, he was fatally injured in a collision.

Alec M'Nair, who joined us in 1904 shortly after
Dan Doyle's retiral, must be bracketed with the latter
as the outstanding defender of his day.

Like Dowds, M'Nair was versatile and played in
several positions for us before settling down as our
regular right back.

Previous to coming to Parkhead M'Nair played for
Stenhousemuir, being a native of that district, and in
my first interview I was greatly impressed with his
sincerity and his upright character.

F 2

He was not long with us before I felt convinced that in him we had a treasure and a gentleman in every sense of the word. His place in the team was quickly assured, and in his twenty years' service I had never once reason to alter my first impression of him. He was the coolest and most intelligent and thoughtful player I have ever seen. Nothing disturbed him, and in our keenest tussles and most exciting experiences he maintained an unruffled demeanour. A most popular fellow in every company, Alec was honoured *v*. England in 1908, 9, 12, 13, 14, 20; *v*. Wales, 1906, 8, 10, 12, 20; *v*. Ireland, 1907, 12, 14, 20; *v*. English League, 1908, 10, 11, 12, 14, 15, 20; *v*. Irish League, 1909, 10, 12, 14, 15; *v*. Southern League, 1913, 14.

Patsy Gallagher. During the fifty years of the Club's existence many brilliant players have played their part in making history and not the least of these was Patsy Gallagher, who many declare was the " finest o' them a' ".

Well, I am not going to express any opinion on that or make comparisons, but I will say, and without any fear of contradiction, that there never was one who gave better service to the Club and with so little to commend him in the way of physique.

When he turned out to play a trial for us at Dumfries in 1911, we had no serious intention of signing him, as his appearance gave no indication of the power and endurance he possessed, not to speak of ability—he was under 5 feet 6 inches and just a little over 7 stones in weight.

Nevertheless we gave him another trial and his

cleverness simply forced us to sign him, although we feared he would never stand up to the wear and tear of League football.

How wrong we were in our estimate was proved by the fact that five months later he had earned a Scottish Cup medal and scored one of the goals which beat Clyde in the final.

The " mighty atom " he was aptly named, full of energy and a master in the art of turning apparent defeat into victory.

Born in Donegal, he was honoured by Ireland fifteen times and once by the Free State—in addition he has 4 Scottish Cup medals, 7 League Championships, 10 Charity Cup and 4 Inter-League medals.

After leaving Celtic he spent five seasons with Falkirk, earning a benefit with that club, Celtic supplying the opposition.

Jimmy McGrory joined Celtic in season 1922-3. His ambition as a boy was to become a Celt when he grew up. We were first told about him when he played in a Boys' Guild team. We kept a watchful eye on him. He stepped into junior football. His club was St. Roch's. Our watchfulness increased. I was struck not by his ball play so much as by his adaptability, his versatility and by his tremendous enthusiasm and virility.

When our time to take Jimmy came, we had no difficulty in making him a Celt. His heart was ours long before he was offered a peg in our dressing-room. He brought with him a fervour and freshness which revealed the real Celtic spirit. He has been a great player for Celtic and for Scotland.

With all respect to the many other splendid Celts we have had and still have, I want to say this: We have never had, unless with one exception, a player whose prowess and o'erflowing enthusiasm have led us to so many brilliant victories. The exception is Paddy Gallagher. As a goal-getter McGrory stands supreme. He has scored more goals with his head than any other player. Celtic have had many offers for his transfer. Arsenal wanted him very much. We left it to him to say " Yes " or " No ". " No " it was. He wanted to finish his playing career with Celtic.

Among the galaxy of talented goalkeepers whom Celtic have had, the late lamented **John Thomson** was the greatest. A Fifeshire friend recommended him to the Club. We watched him play. We were impressed so much that we signed him when he was still in his teens. That was in 1926. Next year he became our regular goalkeeper, and was soon regarded as one of the finest goalkeepers in the country.

But, alas, his career was to be short. In September, 1931, playing against Rangers at Ibrox Park, he met with a fatal accident. Yet he had played long enough to gain the highest honours football had to give. A most likeable lad, modest and unassuming, he was popular wherever he went.

His merit as a goalkeeper shone superbly in his play. Never was there a keeper who caught and held the fastest shots with such grace and ease. In all he did there was balance and beauty of movement wonderful to watch. Among the great Celts who have passed over, he has an honoured place.

A memorial card with a photograph of John Thomson was issued bearing the following inscription:

A Tribute from

WILLIAM MALEY

in proud and loving memory of

JOHN THOMSON

Goalkeeper of the
Celtic Football Club

Who died from injuries accidentally received in saving his goal in a League match between Celtic and Rangers at Ibrox Park, Glasgow, on 5th September, 1931.

" They never die who live in the hearts of those they leave behind."

JOHN THOMSON

Hail and Farewel!! we say of those
  Who come, and pass too soon,
The broken arc, the blasted rose,
  The life cut short ere noon.

Hail and Farewell to you, Dear John,
  More regal than a king,
More graceful than the fleet-limbed fawn,
  Your year ends at its spring.

The athlete rare, who typified
  All that is best in life,
Your brilliant deeds! the death you died!
  Our lovely lad from Fife.

The unerring eye, the master touch;
  More buoyant than the ball!
The fearless heart, the powerful clutch,
  The genius, praised by all.

The squirrel's swift leap, the falcon's flight,
  The clear quick-thinking brain,
All these were yours, for our delight;
  Never, alas! again.

We did not need your death to tell
  You were the sportsman true,
We bow to fate, Hail and Farewell!
  We shall remember you.

Copyright.

T. SMITH
(of Darvel).

The American Tour of 1931

For many long years the Board of the Club had cherished an ambition to tour America, and on numerous occasions were forced to refuse invitations to visit the great republic on the other side of the Atlantic owing to the difficulties to be overcome.

We had no doubt as to the magnificent welcome which awaited us, but there were many other things to be considered and countless obstacles to be surmounted.

Twenty-eight years ago—in 1910 to be exact—Mr. Tom Colgan and myself crossed to New York in order to try and come to some arrangement which would permit Celtic to satisfy the craving of so many exiles who longed to see the game played as it ought to be played—those who probably when in the old country were staunch supporters of other clubs, but knew full well that we would uphold not only our own reputation, but that of Scottish football.

Our journey was a fruitless one. Many there were, as I have said, who wanted to greet us, but Association football was not at that time popular enough to induce the sports over there to make our journey a paying one, and so the idea was dropped for the time being.

In 1930, however, negotiations were opened up with us, and in May of the following year a very happy party boarded the *Caledonia* en route for the " Shores of Amerikay ".

Four of the directors, Messrs. T. White, J. Kelly, T. Colgan, and J. McKillop, accompanied the party with myself and seventeen players, who were as follows:

J. Thomson, W. Cook, W. M'Gonagle, J. Morrison, P. Wilson, J. M'Stay, C. Geatons, R. Whitelaw, D. Currie, W. Hughes, R. Thomson, A. Thomson, J. M'Grory, P. Scarff, C. Napier, J. M'Ghee and H. Smith.

On the journey across the Atlantic the directors had a very happy thought. Recalling that my brother Tom was so very closely identified with the inception of the Club and played such a prominent part in its early struggles, they decided to invite him to join the party, and he crossed in the next steamer which sailed a week later.

Our voyage was not a very pleasant one, heavy seas and fog being encountered most of the time, but in due course we landed in New York on 22nd May, and received a splendid reception.

Throughout the whole tour indeed we received great kindness and hospitality, in fact our hosts couldn't do enough for us—our journey was just like a royal procession, and in passing I might just remark that all the fêting and " receptioning " was not exactly conducive to good condition in a football sense.

We had won the Scottish Cup a month earlier, and carried it with us throughout our tour. Words cannot describe how a sight of the trophy affected those exiles to whom it recalled many memories of home.

Not once, but on many occasions, I saw tears run down the cheeks of those who actually fought their way through the crowds to get a close view of it, as they gazed with a feeling almost amounting to reverence.

As this was the first occasion on which the Scottish Cup had been seen in America, it is easy to imagine the enthusiasm the sight of it being carried round the fields evoked, and the " auld Scots sangs " that were sung as if to increase the warmth of its welcome.

We were not given much time to stretch our legs after leaving the *Caledonia*, as on the following day we met Pennsylvania All Stars, whom we defeated by 6–1.

Our reception in this game—at Philadelphia—was simply wonderful. The people couldn't do enough for us, and I have no hesitation in saying that no other place even approached Philadelphia for the kindnesses and attentions showered upon us all.

Returning to New York we faced the New York Giants on the following day, winning by 3–2, but by the time we played our next game, six days later, the players were not in such good fettle.

The terrific heat had begun to tell on them—the food was strange and generally unsuitable from their point of view, and when you add to these discomforts the continued strain of meeting friends and relations of friends which entailed conversations and celebrations, innocent though they were, it will be realized that they were not just 100 per cent. This was responsible for our first defeat, the New York Yankees beating us by 4–3—a different tale was told when we met the same team two days before we sailed for home.

By that time the men were acclimatized and made ample atonement for their earlier defeat as, playing magnificent football, they beat the " Yankees " by 4–1.

As may be imagined the grounds were our greatest handicap, and in certain towns the accommodation would have disgraced a juvenile club.

Pawtucket was easily the worst we encountered. The ground was like a furnace, dressing conditions disgraceful, the referee had no control whatever, permitting some fearfully rough play in the game.

The win-at-all-cost element was met with very often, and I noticed particularly that the defenders were as a rule the most unscrupulous.

Perhaps the most exciting match of the tour was witnessed at Fall River, where we lost by 1–0. We have cause to remember that game as it was to our present goalkeeper, Joe Kennaway, that we owed our defeat.

At that time he was playing for Fall River, and his display was simply marvellous; indeed with an ordinary keeper opposed to us on that occasion we would have won with a few to spare.

Well, we have no reason to regret the experience, as after poor John Thomson met with his tragic death, and we were looking for someone to fill his place, my mind went back to the Fall River match and the display of Kennaway.

I immediately set about getting into touch with him, and as quickly as he could get away Kennaway crossed to Glasgow to become a Celt.

After our reverse at Pawtucket the players seemed to get the hang of things as on the following day they beat Brooklyn by 5–0, and six days later defeated Carsteel by 7–0.

Next day they ran up against something entirely new. They were by this time fairly well accustomed to the rough-and-ready conditions and to the inefficient referees, but the Hakoah lot were a different proposition.

This team, I think, was made up of Jews, not that it made any difference, of course, but they appeared to have a way with them, as the referee did whatever he was told.

M'Grory had his jaw fractured, but nobody seemed to worry over the fact. Then for some reason quite unknown to the visitors, Napier was ordered off.

It was not an enjoyable experience for any of us, least of all M'Grory, but we kept our end up, the game finishing 1–1.

Five games were played after this, all of which were won, but we were all very tired and weary when we boarded the steamer for home.

Still, we all extracted great satisfaction and enjoyment from the tour, the former because we felt that we had brought Scotland a little nearer to many who had hoped, but never really expected to see, the day when a Scots team should play in America.

I met many men and women, too, who had travelled hundreds of miles just to see us play, although there were, of course, many others who were anxious to meet some of our party—fathers who insisted on introducing their sons born in America probably to some of the old-timers they remembered years before.

Although all this happened only seven years ago, it is rather sad to recall that five of the party have since passed away: James Kelly, Tom E. Maley, John Thomson, Peter Scarff, and R. Thomson.

To those of us who remain it will always be a consoling thought that the five who are gone participated in one of the greatest adventures of the Celtic Club.

RESULTS OF GAMES PLAYED

May 23.	Pennsylvania All Stars	..	6–1
,, 24.	New York Giants	.. ..	3–2
,, 30.	New York Yankees	.. ..	3–4
,, 31.	Fall River	.. ..	0–1
June 6.	Pawtucket Rangers	.. ..	1–3
,, 7.	Brooklyn	.. ..	5–0
,, 13.	Carsteel	.. ..	7–0
,, 14.	Hakoah	.. ..	1–1
,, 21.	Bricklayers	.. ..	6–3
,, 25.	Michigan All Stars	.. ..	5–0
,, 27.	Ulster United ..	.. ..	3–1
,, 28.	New York Yankees	.. ..	4–1
,, 29.	Baltimore	.. ..	4–1

Played 13. Won 9. Lost 3. Drawn 1.

Goals for, 48.   Goals against, 18.

Jubilee Dinner

Wednesday, 16th June, 1938

REPORT OF PROCEEDINGS

Representatives of football interests in Scotland, England and Ireland were present in the Grosvenor Restaurant, Glasgow, to celebrate the Jubilee of the Celtic Football Club. Distinguished legislators, club representatives, and famous players, past and present, assembled to pay tribute to the achievements of the Club during the fifty years of its existence and the wonderful contribution it had made to Scottish sport.

On display at the banquet were the Exhibition Cup of 1902, the Glasgow Charity Cup, the Shield presented to Celtic by the Scottish Football Association in recognition of their feat of winning the Scottish League Championship six seasons in succession, and the Exhibition Trophy won by the club during the previous week.

Mr. Wm. Maley, manager of the Club, who has been associated with the Club since the team was formed, as player and manager, also celebrated his football jubilee, and the Club showed its appreciation of his services by presenting him with a cheque for 2500 guineas, equivalent to 50 guineas for each year of service.

Mr. Tom White, chairman of the Club, presided over the banquet.

The toast of " The Club " was proposed by Sir John T. Cargill, hon. president of the Rangers Football Club and the Glasgow Merchants' Charity Cup Committee.

He recalled that he had proposed the toast of the Rangers F.C. at the Jubilee Dinner, and said he was now proud to have a similar honour at Celtic's Jubilee gathering. Rangers and Celtic had been great rivals, but they were also great friends. He had seen many good matches between them.

Celtic was founded in 1888 by Brother Walfrid, a Marist Brother, who, along with other clergymen in the East End of Glasgow, ran free breakfasts for the poor people of that area. In 1887 the Hibs had won the Scottish Cup, and Brother Walfrid and Mr. John Glass came to the conclusion that it would be a good thing to start an Irish team in Glasgow to raise funds for the free breakfasts. That was the start of the Club, and it had nobly done the work that was begun 50 years ago.

Celtic Football Club was an Irish club, and one of the great characteristics of the Irish race was not only their generosity and large-heartedness but they were the greatest sportsmen in the world. They took an interest in every sport, and played every sport magnificently as only Irishmen could.

Those men did not know much about football, and they called in experts, the brothers Maley. Tom, who was a schoolmaster, played for Partick Thistle, Third Lanark and Hibernians. Mr. Wm. Maley was a junior then.

He started off in 1888 as match secretary to Celtic. He played for them, and was still going strong. Celtic thought they could do what Hibernians had done, but they also thought they would get some assistance from Hibernians, and they secured five of their players. They also got two of the famous Renton. They started off by beating Rangers 5–2, and then they went into the final of the Scottish Cup to be beaten by Third Lanark. So on for 50 years, more or less, at the top of the tree were Celtic the wonderful club, and one they could all be proud of.

When one looked back over the players of those 50 years, one thought of names like Doyle, M'Mahon, Kelly, Quinn, Hay, Young, M'Menemy, Somers, Adams, M'Nally, Gallagher, Shaw, Dodds, and poor John Thomson, who laid his life down for his club; M'Gonagle, the brothers M'Stay, M'Farlane, and the great M'Grory, who held the record for goals in first-class football—540.

Referring to the management of the Club, Sir John said Mr. White had been for 30 years a member of the Club and 20 years chairman. He had also been the president of the Scottish Football Association. He had brought to the football world a delightfully breezy manner which had made him and his Club so popular. They had still the oldest member of the Club, Mr. Tom Colgan. He had been for 34 years a member of the committee and was still going strong.

Then they had Mr. Maley, who answered the description, in a way, of the strong but not silent man. He was a strong man with strong views, but one needed that to succeed as manager of a football club.

In giving the toast, he wished, as they all did, continued success for an unlimited number of years, and he was sure that so long as Association football was played, so

long would the Celtic Club be in the van, and would be
looked up to, respected, and loved by the followers of the
game.

Before the toast was honoured the company sang " The
Dear Little Shamrock ".

Mr. White briefly acknowledged the toast, and thanked
Sir John for his eloquent tribute to the Club.

In making the presentation to Mr. Maley, Mr. White
said the Club manager had celebrated his 70th birthday
the other day. Of these 70 years, 50 had been spent in
the service of the Celtic Club, and they would be very
unmindful of what they owed to him if they did not mark
the occasion by making him some form of presentation.

The triumphs of the Celtic Club were the triumphs of
Mr. Maley, whose life had been indissolubly allied to Celtic.

In these 50 years he had carried out his managerial
duties in a wonderful manner.

He had reared his own players, blended them, and
moulded them into a specific style of footballer, the equal
of anything in the whole country.

He had blazed a trail of football round the Continent
and in America. Everywhere he went he was received
with the courtesy and attention shown to the ambassadors
of his country.

The name of Maley was synonymous with the Celtic
Club, and almost with the name of soccer.

He had also done a great deal of work for football
generally. He had been a legislator for many years, and
his advice had been warmly accepted by members of
leagues and associations in these islands.

As a token of the respect and regard they had for

many years for Mr. Maley he desired to present him with a cheque for 2500 guineas.

Mr. William Maley, acknowledging the presentation, said he was deeply grateful to Mr. White for the many nice things he had said about him and to the company for the generous support they had given to the sentiments expressed by the chairman of the Club.

He considered his first duty on the greatest day of his life was to return grateful thanks to Almighty God for His goodness and guidance over the 70 years of his life, and especially during the 50 years which he had spent with the Celtic Club, in his wanderings for it all over the world. He may not have been blessed with wealth, but he had been favoured with the greatest asset for man in life—good health.

During the long stretch of his connexion with the Club this was the first benefit he had received, and he was indebted to the Board that they had made it one worthy of the great occasion and of the Celtic Club, which had always done things in a big way.

Celtic started off in their first year doing what no other Scottish club had ever done—played in the Scottish Cup Final. They were the first club to extend their ground for international attendance purposes. Celtic were also pioneers in the installation of telegraphic accommodation for the Press.

They were the first team to visit the Continent, and also the first club to build a double-decker stand for the convenience of the spectators.

In addition, they were the first club to play two games in one day—and won both.

Celtic led the way in bringing to Scotland all the athletic stars of the world, and did so for many years. They were the first team to have a " strike ", and join with another famous club the first riot at a final. (Laughter.)

Words could not fully express his feelings, and all he could say was that what he had done for the Celtic Club in the past he would gladly do again. It had been a labour of love, and he hoped when he was gone his successor would lend to his work the enthusiasm and love of the Club which had been almost a craze with him.

Mr. Maley expressed regret at the absence through illness of the last surviving member of the first Celtic Committee, Mr. Joe Nelis. They had with them, how- ever, two of their oldest enthusiasts, Dr. Scanlan and Mrs. Arthur Murphy, who had been with them from the very beginning.

On such an occasion, continued Mr. Maley, they must not forget some of the men who started the Celtic Club on its grand career and who had done much for it in the early days. Of the old brigade, there were two names which could not be forgotten by anyone who had followed the Club's work. They were Brother Walfrid, the founder of the Club, and John Glass, his lieutenant and the Celtic president for many years.

Without those two men the Club would never have survived in the early days as the funds were low and the opposition of a section of the public very strong. Both men, however, were fighters, and so the Club gradually found its feet and was duly launched to achieve the success it did in its first year and which led to the great heights of later years.

There were, of course, many more who also helped in the good work, and to those old-timers who were still to the fore the names of J. H. M'Laughlin, Frank M'Erlean, Tom Maley, James M'Kay, Hugh Darroch, Dr. Conway, Wm. M'Killop, John M'Killop, Michael Hughes, Joseph Shaughnessy, Dan Malloy, James Curtis and John O'Hare would revive memories.

The formation of the Club into a limited company, which was found essential for its future welfare, created a new form of management. Many on the Board had gone, but they still had old directors with them who had served for over thirty years in the persons of Mr. Tom White and Mr. Tom Colgan.

Mr. White had joined the Board in 1908, and was elected chairman in 1914—a position he had held ever since. Mr. White, as the youngest of the Board when he joined, brought to the Club's service the enthusiasm of youth, which, harnessed to the old traditions, had made for the great success it had achieved. He had also been a great asset to Scottish football, and the game was all the poorer when he left the chair of the S.F.A. which he had filled ably and well for six years.

The oldest surviving director was Mr. Tom Colgan, who had been with the Club since its earliest days and joined the Board of Directors in 1904. Of a quiet disposition, Mr. Colgan had been of great service to the Club.

The first team that played for Celtic was in a game against their great rivals of to-day, Rangers, whom they defeated at Celtic Park on 27th May, 1888, by 5 goals to 2. The names of the men who played in that game were worthy of mention — Michael Dolan (Drumpellier),

E. Pearson (Carfin), J. M'Laughlin (Govan Whitefield), W. Maley (Cathcart), James Kelly (Renton), P. Murray (Blantyre), Neil M'Callum (Renton), T. E. Maley (Third Lanark), John Madden (Dumbarton), M. Dunbar (Cartvale Busby), H. M'Govern (Govan Hibs). Of that lot, only Madden, who had been in Prague as a coach for thirty years, and himself (Mr. Maley) were alive. He (Mr. Maley) represented the last of the first office-bearers.

In 1931, when the Club had fulfilled a long-cherished dream of visiting and playing in America and Canada, he had had a photograph taken one day of the three survivors of the earliest team of 1888–89—James Kelly, Tom Maley and himself—little dreaming that in the jubilee festivities they were even then looking forward to he alone would be left of the men who had set the good ship Celtic on its great career. Of the old players, they had present the oldest in service after himself—John Kelly, who kept goal for Celtic for a period in 1889. Another old friend with them was James Bell, of Mauchline, who kept goal for Celtic in 1890 when they won the Glasgow Cup—the first big trophy the Club had won. They, of course, had won the North-eastern Cup earlier, but that competition was confined to a section of the city.

Time did not permit of him mentioning all the great players who had adorned the Celtic colours, but the names of such as Doyle, M'Mahon, James Kelly, Tom Maley, P. Gallagher, M'Laren, Groves, M'Keown, M'Callum, Quinn, Orr, Hay, Young, Loney, M'Nair, Dodds, M'Menemy, Welford, Battles, Divers, M'Arthur, Campbell, M'Grory, John Thomson, M'Stay, M'Lean, M'Inally, Cassidy, Buchan, the O'Donnells, Napier, down to the present list, should tell all enthusiasts for the game of the many football giants Celtic had brought out to do credit to their Club and country.

During all the years it had been a great source of pride to him to know that the players who had worn their colours had never ceased in their interest in the fortunes of the old Club. It was, therefore, a great pleasure for him to see so many of them present and to know that they still retained the kindly feelings they always had for himself.

In all his work as a manager, Mr. Maley said he had always felt it his duty to put the success of the Club first in his dealings with players, but he felt sure there was no player who thought that that duty was ever used against his success or welfare.

Club managers were apt to be misunderstood by people who should know better. The club which employed a manager expected of him service for the benefit of the club all the time, and when it ran contrary to the desires of individuals the manager invariably got the blame. That, however, had never worried him, nor should it trouble any genuine servant of a club.

Mr. Maley said he believed he had travelled about 300,000 miles over Britain and the Continents of Europe and America in his fifty years of football life.

To the Celtic Board he extended his sincere thanks for their courtesy and help at all times, and even forbearance when his personal enthusiasm may have led him into some indiscretions. They knew all the time that it was just his old Irish heart beating too fast, and that it was all meant for the best.

He was very proud of the fact that never had there

been any club manager with such complete liberty of action or fullness of power as the Celtic Management had accorded to him, and in all his years with them he had never betrayed that faith.

They had made him extremely happy, and he would never forget that great occasion or the people who had made it such a memorable one.

Brother Germanus proposed the toast of the Corporation of Glasgow, and made reference to Brother Walfrid's association with the Celtic Club.

The Lord Provost, Sir John Stewart, in his reply, recalled that he had been present at the opening of the Parkhead ground by Celtic 50 years ago.

Col. John Shaughnessy toasted " Our Guests ", and Mr. Tom Reid (chairman of Partick Thistle) responded.

Mr. James Bowie, of Rangers Football Club, toasted the chairman.

Internationals Played at Celtic Park

Scotland v. England

1894.	Draw, 2–2	..	..	..	Gate drawings £2071
1896.	Scotland won, 2–1	..	..	,,	,, £2440
1898.	England won, 3–1	..	..	,,	,, £1907
1900.	Scotland won, 4–1	..	..	,,	,, £2717
1904.	England won, 1–0	..	..	,,	,, £1942

Scotland v. Wales

1914. Draw, 0–0.

Scotland v. Ireland

				Scotland.		Ireland.
1890–91.	28th March, 1891	..	..	2	..	1
1892–93.	25th March, 1893	..	..	6	..	1
1894–95.	30th March, 1895	..	..	3	..	1
1898–99.	25th March, 1899	..	..	9	..	1
1900–01.	2nd March, 1901	..	..	11	..	0
1902–03.	21st March, 1903	..	..	0	..	2
1904–05.	18th March, 1905	..	..	4	..	0
1906–07.	16th March, 1907	..	..	3	..	0
1910–11.	18th March, 1911	..	..	2	..	0
1919–20.	13th March, 1920	..	..	3	..	0
1921–22.	4th March, 1922	..	..	2	..	1
1923–24.	1st March, 1924	..	..	2	..	0
1929–30.	22nd Feb., 1930	..	..	3	..	1
1933–34.	16th Sept., 1933	..	..	1	..	2

Scottish League v. English League

1892–93.	England 4, Scotland 3	..	Gate takings,	£728
1894–95.	,, 4 ,, 3	..	,,	£1096
1898–99.	,, 4 ,, 1	..	,,	£1275
1902–03.	,, 3 ,, 0	..	,,	£1460
1908–09.	,, 1 ,, 3	..	,,	£1530
1914–15.	,, 4 ,, 1	..	,,	£1656
1925–26.	,, 2 ,, 0	..	,,	£3130
1931–32.	,, 3 ,, 4	..	,,	£3400

Scottish League v. Irish League

1893–94.	Scotland 6, Ireland 2.
1895–96.	,, 3 ,, 2.
1922–23	,, 3 ,, 0.

Celtic's Scottish Cup Record

1888–89

Round		Opponents		Ground
First round.	5.	Shettleston,	1.	Celtic Park.
Second round.	8.	Cowlairs,	0.	Celtic Park.
Third round.	4.	Albion Rovers,	1.	Celtic Park.
Fourth round.	4.	St. Bernard,	1.	Edinburgh.
Fifth round.	0.	Clyde,	1.	Celtic Park.
Fifth round. (protested tie).	9.	Clyde,	2.	Celtic Park.
Sixth round.	2.	East Stirling,	1.	Falkirk.
Semi-final.	4.	Dumbarton,	1.	Dumbarton.
Final.	0.	Third Lanark,	3.	Hampden.
Final.	1.	Third Lanark,	2.	Hampden.

1889–90

Round		Opponents		Ground
First round.	0.	Queen's Park,	0.	Celtic Park.
Replay.	1.	Queen's Park,	2.	Hampden.

1890–91

Round		Opponents		Ground
First round.	1.	Rangers,	0.	Celtic Park.
Second round.	2.	Carfin Shamrock,	2.	Celtic Park.
Replay.	3.	Carfin Shamrock,	1.	Carfin.
Third round.	6.	Wishaw Thistle,	2.	Wishaw.
Fourth round.	3.	Our Boys,	1.	Dundee.
Fifth round. (game stopped).	4.	Royal Albert,	0.	Larkhall.
Replay.	2.	Royal Albert,	0.	Ibrox Park.
Semi-final.	0.	Dumbarton,	3.	Dumbarton.

1891-92

Round		Opponents		Ground
First round.	4.	St. Mirren,	2.	Paisley.
Second round.	3.	Kilmarnock Ath.,	0.	Celtic Park.
Third round.	4.	Cowlairs,	1.	Celtic Park.
Semi-final.	5.	Rangers,	3.	Celtic Park.
Final.	1.	Queen's Park,	0.	Ibrox Park.
(Friendly game.)				
Final.	5.	Queen's Park,	1.	Ibrox Park.

1892-93

First round.	3.	Linthouse,	1.	Celtic Park.
Second round.	8.	5th K.R.V.,	0.	Celtic Park.
Third round.	5.	3rd L.R.V.,	1.	Celtic Park.
Semi-final.	5.	St. Bernard,	0.	Celtic Park.
Final.	1.	Queen's Park,	2.	Ibrox Park.

1893-94

First round.	6.	Hurlford,	0.	Celtic Park.
Second round.	7.	Albion Rovers,	0.	Celtic Park.
Third round.	8.	St. Bernard,	1.	Celtic Park.
Semi-final.	5.	Third Lanark,	3.	Cathkin Park.
Final.	1.	Rangers,	3.	Hampden Park

1894-95

First round.	4.	Queen's Park,	1.	Celtic Park.
Second round.	0.	Hibernian,	2.	Edinburgh.
Second round.	2.	Hibernian,	0.	Edinburgh.
Third round.	0.	Dundee,	1.	Dens Park.

1895-96

First round.	2.	Queen's Park,	4.	Celtic Park.

1896-97

First round.	2.	Arthurlie,	4.	Barrhead.

1897–98

Round		Opponents		Ground
First round.	7.	Arthurlie,	0.	Barrhead.
Second round.	2.	Third Lanark,	3.	Cathkin Park.

1898–99

First round.	8.	6th G.R.V.,	1.	Dalbeattie.
Second round.	3.	St. Bernard,	0.	Celtic Park.
Third round.	4.	Queen's Park,	2.	Hampden Park.
	2.	Queen's Park,	1.	Celtic Park.
Semi-final.	4.	Port Glasgow,	2.	Celtic Park.
Final.	2.	Rangers,	0.	Hampden Park.

1899–1900

First round.	7.	Bo'ness,	1.	Celtic Park.
Second round.	5.	Port-Glasgow,	1.	Port-Glasgow.
Third round.	4.	Kilmarnock,	1.	Celtic Park.
Semi-final.	2.	Rangers,	2.	Ibrox Park.
Replay.	4.	Rangers.	0.	Celtic Park.
Final.	4.	Queen's Park,	3.	Ibrox Park.

1900–01

First round.	1.	Rangers,	0.	Celtic Park.
Second round.	6.	Kilmarnock,	0.	Celtic Park.
Third round.	1.	Dundee,	0.	Dens Park.
Semi-final.	1.	St. Mirren,	0.	Celtic Park.
Final.	3.	Hearts,	4.	Ibrox Park.

1901–02

First round.	3.	Thornliebank,	0.	Celtic Park.
Second round.	3.	Arbroath,	2.	Arbroath.
Third round.	1.	Hearts,	1.	Tynecastle.
Replay.	2.	Hearts,	1.	Celtic Park.
Semi-final.	3.	St. Mirren,	2.	Paisley.
Final.	0.	Hibernian,	1.	Celtic Park.

1902–03

Round		Opponents		Ground
First round.	0.	St. Mirren,	0.	Celtic Park.
Replay.	1.	St. Mirren,	1.	Paisley.
Replay.	1.	St. Mirren,	0.	*Ibrox.
Replay.	4.	St. Mirren,	0.	Ibrox.
Second round.	2.	Port-Glasgow,	0.	Celtic Park.
Third round.	0.	Rangers,	3.	Celtic Park.

* Stopped midway through second half owing to weather.

1903–04

Round		Opponents		Ground
First round.	4.	St. Bernard,	0.	
Second round.	1.	Dundee,	1.	Celtic Park.
Replay.	0.	Dundee,	0.	Dens Park.
Replay.	5.	Dundee,	0.	Celtic Park.
Semi-final.	2.	Third Lanark,	1.	Celtic Park.
Final.	3.	Rangers,	2.	Hampden Park.

1904–05

Round		Opponents		Ground
First round.	2.	Dumfries,	1.	Dumfries.
Second round.	3.	Lochgelly Un.,	0.	Celtic Park.
Third round.	3.	Partick Thistle,	0.	Celtic Park.
Fourth round.	0.	Rangers,	2.	Celtic Park.

1905–06

Round		Opponents		Ground
First round.	2.	Dundee,	1.	Dens Park.
Second round.	3.	Bo'ness,	0.	Celtic Park.
Third round.	1.	Hearts,	2.	Celtic Park.

1906–07

Round		Opponents		Ground
First round.	2.	Clyde,	1.	Celtic Park.
Second round.	0.	Morton,	0.	Greenock.
Replay.	1.	Morton,	1.	Celtic Park.
Replay.	2.	Morton,	1.	Celtic Park.
Third round.	3.	Rangers,	0.	Ibrox Park.
Semi-final.	0.	Hibernian,	0.	Celtic Park.
Replay.	0.	Hibernian,	0.	Easter Road.
Replay.	3.	Hibernian,	0.	Celtic Park.
Final.	3.	Hearts,	0.	Hampden Park.

1907–08

Round		Opponents		Ground
First round.	4.	Peebles Rovers,	0.	Celtic Park.
Second round.	2.	Rangers,	1.	Ibrox Park.
Third round.	3.	Raith Rovers,	0.	Kirkcaldy.
Semi-final.	1.	Aberdeen,	0.	Aberdeen.
Final.	5.	St. Mirren,	1.	Hampden Park.

1908–09

Round		Opponents		Ground
First round.	4.	Leith Athletic,	2.	Leith.
Second round.	4.	Port-Glasgow,	0.	Celtic Park.
Third round.	3.	Airdrieonians,	1.	Celtic Park.
Semi-final.	0.	Clyde,	0.	Celtic Park.
Replay.	2.	Clyde,	0.	Celtic Park.
Final.	2.	Rangers,	2.	Hampden Park.
Replay.	1.	Rangers,	1.	Hampden Park.
(Cup withheld.)				

1909–10

Round		Opponents		Ground
First round.	2.	Dumbarton,	1.	Dumbarton.
Second round.	3.	Third Lanark,	1.	Celtic Park.
Third round.	2.	Aberdeen,	1.	Celtic Park.
Fourth round.	1.	Clyde,	3.	Shawfield Park.

1910–11

Round		Opponents		Ground
First round.	2.	St. Mirren,	0.	Celtic Park.
Second round.	1.	Galston,	0.	Celtic Park.
Third round.	1.	Clyde,	0.	Celtic Park.
Semi-final.	1.	Aberdeen,	0.	Celtic Park.
Final.	0.	Hamilton Acas.,	0.	Ibrox Park.
Replay.	2.	Hamilton Acas.,	0.	Ibrox Park.

‘1911–12

First round.	1.	Dunfermline Ath.,	0.	Celtic Park.
Second round.	3.	East Stirlingshire,	0.	Celtic Park.
Third round.	2.	Aberdeen,	2.	Aberdeen.
Replay.	2.	Aberdeen,	0.	Celtic Park.
Semi-final.	3.	Hearts,	0.	Ibrox Park.
Final.	2.	Clyde,	0.	Ibrox Park.

1912–13

First round.	4.	Arbroath,	0.	Celtic Park.
Second round.	3.	Peebles Rovers,	0.	Celtic Park.
Third round.	0.	Hearts,	1.	Celtic Park.

1913–14

First round.	0.	Clyde,	0.	Shawfield Park.
Replay.	2.	Clyde.	0.	Celtic Park.
Second round.	5.	Forfar Ath.,	0.	Forfar.
Third round.	3.	Motherwell,	1.	Motherwell.
Semi-final.	2.	Third Lanark,	0.	Cathkin Park.
Final.	0.	Hibernian,	0.	Ibrox Park.
Replay.	4.	Hibernian,	1.	Ibrox Park.

1914–19

(No Competition)

1919–20

Round		Opponents		Ground
First round.	3.	Dundee,	1.	Dundee.
Second round.	2.	Partick Thistle,	0.	Celtic Park.
Third round.	0.	Rangers,	1.	Ibrox Park.

1920–21

First round.	3.	Vale of Leven,	0.	Alexandria.
Second round.	3.	East Fife,	1.	Methil.
Third round.	1.	Hearts,	2.	Celtic Park.

1921–22

First round.	4.	Montrose,	0.	Celtic Park.
Second round.	1.	Third Lanark,	0.	Cathkin Park.
Third round.	1.	Hamilton Acas.,	3.	Celtic Park.

1922–23

First round.	3.	Lochgelly Un.,	2.	Lochgelly.
Second round.	4.	Hurlford,	0.	Celtic Park.
Third round.	2.	East Fife,	1.	Celtic Park.
Fourth round.	1.	Raith Rovers,	0.	Celtic Park.
Semi-final.	2.	Motherwell,	0.	Ibrox Park.
Final.	1.	Hibernian,	0.	Hampden Park.

1923–24

First round.	0.	Kilmarnock,	2.	Kilmarnock.

1924–25

First round.	5.	Third Lanark,	1.	Cathkin Park.
Second round.	2.	Alloa Athletic,	1.	Celtic Park.
Third round.	2.	Solway Star,	0.	Celtic Park.
Fourth round.	0.	St. Mirren,	0.	Paisley.
Replay.	1.	St. Mirren,	1.	Celtic Park.
Replay.	1.	St. Mirren,	0.	Ibrox Park.
Semi-final.	5.	Rangers,	0.	Hampden Park.
Final.	2.	Dundee,	1.	Hampden Park.

1925–26

Round		Opponents		Ground
First round.	5.	Kilmarnock,	0.	Kilmarnock.
Second round.	4.	Hamilton Acas.,	0.	Celtic Park.
Third round.	4.	Hearts,	0.	Tynecastle.
Fourth round.	6.	Dumbarton,	1.	Celtic Park.
Semi-final,	2.	Aberdeen,	1.	Tynecastle.
Final.	0.	St. Mirren,	2.	Hampden Park.

1926–27

First round.	0.	Queen of the South,	0.	Dumfries.
Replay.	4.	Queen of the South,	1.	Celtic Park.
Second round.	6.	Brechin City,	3.	Brechin.
Third round.	4.	Dundee,	2.	Dundee.
Fourth round.	5.	Bo'ness,	2.	Bo'ness.
Semi-final.	1.	Falkirk,	0.	Ibrox Park.
Final.	3.	East Fife,	1.	Hampden Park.

1927–28

First round.	3.	Bathgate,	1.	Celtic Park.
Second round.	6.	Keith,	1.	Keith.
Third round.	2.	Alloa Athletic,	0.	Celtic Park.
Fourth round.	2.	Motherwell,	0.	Motherwell
Semi-final.	2.	Queen's Park,	1.	Ibrox Park.
Final.	0.	Rangers,	4.	Hampden Park.

1928–29

First round.	5.	Arthurlie,	1.	Celtic Park.
Second round.	3.	East Stirlingshire,	0.	Celtic Park.
Third round.	4.	Arbroath,	1.	Celtic Park.
Fourth round.	0.	Motherwell,	0.	Celtic Park.
Replay.	2.	Motherwell,	1.	Motherwell.
Semi-final.	0.	Kilmarnock,	1.	Ibrox Park.

1929–30

Round		Opponents		Ground
First round.	6.	Inverness Caledonian,	0.	Inverness.
Second round.	5.	Arbroath,	0.	Celtic Park.
Third round.	1.	St. Mirren,	3.	Celtic Park.

1930–31

First round.	2.	East Fife,	1.	Methil.
Second round.	3.	Dundee United,	2.	Dundee.
Third round.	4.	Morton,	1.	Greenock.
Fourth round.	4.	Aberdeen,	0.	Celtic Park.
Semi-final.	3.	Kilmarnock,	0.	Hampden Park.
Final.	2.	Motherwell,	2.	Hampden Park.
Replay.	4.	Motherwell,	2.	Hampden Park.

1931–32

First round.	3.	Falkirk,	2.	Celtic Park.
Second round.	4.	St. Johnstone,	2.	Perth.
Third round.	0.	Motherwell,	2.	Motherwell.

1932–33

First round.	7.	Dunfermline Ath.,	1.	Dunfermline.
Second round.	2.	Falkirk,	0.	Celtic Park.
Third round.	2.	Partick Thistle,	1.	Celtic Park.
Fourth round.	1.	Albion Rovers,	1.	Coatbridge.
Replay.	3.	Albion Rovers,	1.	Celtic Park.
Semi-final.	0.	Hearts,	0.	Hampden Park.
Replay.	2.	Hearts,	1.	Hampden Park.
Final.	1.	Motherwell,	0.	Hampden Park.

1933–34

First round.	6.	Dalbeattie Star,	0.	Dalbeattie.
Second round.	3.	Ayr United,	2.	Ayr.
Third round.	3.	Falkirk,	1.	Celtic Park.
Fourth round.	0.	St. Mirren,	2.	Paisley.

1934-35

Round		Opponents		Ground
First round.	4.	Montrose,	1.	Celtic Park.
Second round.	1.	Partick Thistle,	1.	Celtic Park.
Replay.	3.	Partick Thistle,	1.	Firhill Park.
Third round.		A Bye.		
Fourth round.	1.	Aberdeen,	3.	Aberdeen.

1935-36

First round.		Berwick Rangers Scratched.		
Second round.	1.	St. Johnstone,	2.	Celtic Park.

1936-37

First round.	1.	Stenhousemuir,	1.	Larbert.
Replay.	2.	Stenhousemuir,	0.	Celtic Park.
Second round.	5.	Albion Rovers,	2.	Coatbridge.
Third round.	3.	East Fife,	0.	Methil.
Fourth round.	4.	Motherwell,	4.	Celtic Park.
Replay.	2.	Motherwell,	1.	Motherwell.
Semi-final.	2.	Clyde,	0.	Ibrox Park.
Final.	2.	Aberdeen,	1.	Hampden Park.

1937-38

First round.	2.	Third Lanark,	1.	Cathkin Park.
Second round.	5.	Nithsdale Wands.,	0.	Celtic Park.
Third round.	1.	Kilmarnock,	2.	Celtic Park.

1938-39

First round.	8.	Burntisland,	3.	Burntisland.
Second round.	7.	Montrose,	1.	Montrose.
Third round.	2.	Hearts,	2.	Tynecastle.
Replay.	2.	Hearts,	1.	Celtic Park.
Fourth Round.	1.	Motherwell,	3.	Motherwell.

Glasgow Cup Results Since 1888-89

1888–89
Shettleston (Celtic Park) 11–2.
Rangers (Ibrox), 6–1.
Queen's Park (Celtic Park), 0–2.

1889–90
United Abstainers (Celtic Park), 5–1.
Cambuslang (Celtic Park), 4–1.
Final.
Queen's Park (Cathkin), 2–3.

1890–91
Battlefield (Celtic Park), 7–0.
Northern (Springburn), 2–1.
Clyde (Celtic Park), 5–0.
Partick Thistle (Celtic Park), 5–1.
Final.
Third Lanark (Hampden), 4–0.

1891–92
Kelvinside Athletic (Celtic Park), 11–1.
Partick Thistle (Meadowside), 3–1.
Northern (Celtic Park), 6–0.
Northern (Celtic Park), 3–2. Protested tie.
Linthouse (Celtic Park), 9–2.
Final.
Clyde (Cathkin), 7–1.

1892–93

Pollokshaws (Pollokshaws), 7–2.
Partick Thistle (Meadowside), 2–1.
Partick Thistle (Meadowside), 1–1. Protested tie.
Partick Thistle (Celtic Park), 8–0.
Third Lanark (Celtic Park), 5–2.

Final.

Rangers (Cathkin), 1–3.

1893–94

Linthouse (Govan), 2–1.
Northern (Springburn), 3–2.
Thistle (Glasgow Green), 7–0.
Rangers (Ibrox), 0–1.

1894–95

Battlefield (Celtic Park), 2–2.
Battlefield (Celtic Park), 4–1.
Clyde (Celtic Park), 4–1.
Cowlairs (Springburn), 2–0.

Final.

Rangers (Cathkin), 2–0.

1895–96

Linthouse (Govan), 7–1.
Cambuslang (Celtic Park), 6–1.
Partick Thistle (Celtic Park), 5–1.

Final.

Queen's Park (Ibrox), 6–3.

1896–97

Clyde (Celtic Park), 5–1.
Queen's Park (Hampden), 4–2.

Final.

Rangers (Cathkin), 1–1.
Rangers (Cathkin), 1–2.

1897–98
Clyde (Celtic Park), 2–1.
Rangers (Celtic Park), 2–2.
Rangers (Ibrox), 1–1.
Rangers (Ibrox), 1–3.

1898–99
Clyde (Celtic Park), 7–0.
Rangers (Ibrox), 1–1.
Rangers (Celtic Park), 1–2.

1899–1900
Partick Thistle (Celtic Park), 5–1.
Linthouse (Celtic Park), 5–1.
Final.
Rangers (Cathkin), 1–1.
Rangers (Cathkin), 0–1.

1900–01
Rangers (Ibrox), 3–4.

1901–02
Clyde (Celtic Park), 3–0.
Third Lanark (Celtic Park), 5–1.
Final.
Rangers (Ibrox), 2–2.
Replay (Celtic scratched).

1902–03
Queen's Park (Hampden Park), 2–1.
Clyde (Shawfield), 4–1.
Final.
Third Lanark (Ibrox), 0–3.

1903–04

Queen's Park (Celtic Park), 1–1.
Queen's Park (Hampden), 1–0.
Clyde (Shawfield), 2–0.
Final.
Third Lanark (Ibrox), 1–1.
Third Lanark (Ibrox), 0–1.

1904–05

Queen's Park (Celtic Park), 3–0.
Partick Thistle (Celtic Park), 2–0.
Final.
Rangers (Hampden), 2–1.

1905–06

Queen's Park (Celtic Park), 3–0.
Partick Thistle (Celtic Park), 4–0.
Final.
Third Lanark (Hampden), 3–0.

1906–07

Partick Thistle (Meadowside), 2–0.
Queen's Park (Celtic Park), 5–0.
Final.
Third Lanark (Ibrox), 3–2.

1907–08

Queen's Park (Celtic Park), 2–0.
Final.
Rangers (Hampden), 2–2.
Rangers (Hampden), 0–0.
Rangers (Hampden), 2–1.

1908–09

Queen's Park (Hampden), 4–4.
Queen's Park (Celtic Park), 2–1.
Rangers (Celtic Park), 2–2.
Rangers (Ibrox), 2–0.

Final.

Third Lanark (Hampden), 1–1.
Third Lanark (Hampden), 2–2.
Third Lanark (Hampden), 0–4.

1909–10

Queen's Park (Hampden), 1–1.
Queen's Park (Celtic Park), 6–1.

Final.

Rangers (Hampden), 1–0.

1910–11

Partick Thistle (Firhill), 2–1.
Third Lanark (Celtic Park), 1–0.

Final.

Rangers (Hampden), 1–3.

1911–12

Partick Thistle (Celtic Park), 3–3.
Partick Thistle (Firhill), 0–3.

1912–13

Clyde (Celtic Park), 0–0.
Clyde (Shawfield), 4–0.

Final.

Rangers (Hampden), 1–3.

1913–14

Third Lanark (Celtic Park), 0–0.
Third Lanark (Cathkin), 0–1.

1914–15

Clyde (Shawfield), 0–2.

1915–16

Third Lanark (Celtic Park), 2–0.
Final.
Rangers (Hampden), 2–1.

1916–17

Rangers (Celtic Park), 3–0.
Final.
Clyde (Celtic Park), 3–1.

1917–18

Queen's Park (Hampden), 2–1.
Rangers (Celtic Park), 0–3.

1918–19

Clyde (Celtic Park), 3–1.
Final.
Rangers (Hampden), 0–2.

1919–20

Rangers (Celtic Park), 1–0.
Queen's Park (Celtic Park), 3–1.
Final.
Partick Thistle (Celtic Park), 1–0.

1920–21

Third Lanark (Celtic Park), 3–0.
Rangers (Celtic Park), 2–1.
Final.
Clyde (Celtic Park), 1–0.

1921–22

Queen's Park (Celtic Park), 2–1.
Partick Thistle (Celtic Park), 1–1.
Partick Thistle (Firhill), 2–0.

Final.

Rangers (Hampden), 0–1.

1922–23

Queen's Park (Hampden), 3–4.

1923–24

Rangers (Ibrox), 0–1.

1924–25

Third Lanark (Cathkin), 4–2.

Final.

Rangers (Celtic Park), 1–4.

1925–26

Partick Thistle (Firhill), 1–1.
Partick Thistle (Celtic Park), 5–1.
Rangers (Celtic Park), 2–2.
Rangers (Ibrox), 1–1.
Rangers (Ibrox), 2–0.

Final.

Clyde (Celtic Park), 1–2.

1926–27

Partick Thistle (Celtic Park), 3–1.

Final.

Rangers (Hampden), 1–0.

1927–28
Queen's Park (Hampden), 4–1.
Third Lanark (Celtic Park), 7–0.
Final.
Rangers (Hampden), 2–1.

1928–29
Rangers (Ibrox), 2–1.
Third Lanark (Cathkin), 2–2.
Third Lanark (Celtic Park), 5–1.
Final.
Queen's Park (Hampden), 2–0.

1929–30
Clyde (Shawfield), 1–1.
Clyde (Celtic Park), 6–0.
Queen's Park (Celtic Park), 3–1.
Final.
Rangers (Hampden), 0–0.
Rangers (Hampden), 0–4.

1930–31
Clyde (Shawfield), 3–1.
Final.
Rangers (Hampden), 2–1.

1931–32
Rangers (Celtic Park), 1–1.
Rangers (Ibrox), 2–2.
Rangers (Ibrox), 0–1.

1932–33
Clyde (Shawfield), 1–1.
Clyde (Celtic Park), 3–1.
Partick Thistle (Firhill), 0–1.

1933-34

Third Lanark (Cathkin), 4–1.
Rangers (Celtic Park), 1–1.
Rangers (Ibrox), 1–2.

1934-35

Queen's Park (Celtic Park), 1–0.
Rangers (Celtic Park), 1–2.

1935-36

Third Lanark (Celtic Park), 1–1.
Third Lanark (Cathkin), 1–0.

Final.

Rangers (Ibrox), 0–2.

1936-37

Third Lanark (Cathkin), 3–1.
Rangers (Ibrox), 1–2.

1937-38

Rangers (Celtic Park), 1–2.

1938-39

Third Lanark (Cathkin), 1–1.
Third Lanark (Celtic Park), 8–1.
Queen's Park (Celtic Park), 2–1.

Final.

Clyde (Hampden), 3–0.

Glasgow Charity Cup Results Since 1888-89

1888–89
Renton (Hampden), 2–5.

1889–90
3rd L.R.V. (Hampden), 0–2.

1890–91
LEAGUE CHARITY COMPETITION
3rd L.R.V. (Ibrox), 8–1.
3rd L.R.V. (Celtic Park), 6–1.
Replay owing to protest.
Dumbarton (Cathkin), 0–3.

1891–92
Dumbarton (Ibrox), 3–1.
Final.
Rangers (Celtic Park), 2–0.

1892–93
Dumbarton (Cathkin), 1–1.
Dumbarton (Cathkin), 3–1.
Final.
Rangers (Celtic Park), 5–0.

1893–94
3rd L.R.V. (Hampden), 3–3.
3rd L.R.V. (Hampden), 3–2.
Final.
Queen's Park (Ibrox), 2–1.

1894–95
Queen's Park (Hampden), 1–0.
Final.
Rangers (Cathkin), 4–0.

1895–96
Rangers (Hampden), 6–1.
Final.
Queen's Park (Ibrox), 2–1.

1896–97
Rangers (Hampden), 1–4.

1897–98
Rangers (Cathkin), 0–2.

1898–99
Queen's Park (Cathkin), 4–0.
Final.
Rangers (Ibrox), 2–0.

1899–1900
Queen's Park (Cathkin), 3–2 (unfinished).
Queen's Park (Cathkin), 6–1.
Final.
Rangers (Hampden), 1–5.

1900–01
Rangers (Exhibition), 0–0.
Rangers (Exhibition), 1–0.
Final.
Third Lanark (Exhibition), 0–0.
Third Lanark (Exhibition), 0–3.

1901–02
Hearts (Celtic Park), 3–1.
Third Lanark (Cathkin), 5–0.
Final.
Hibernians (Hampden), 2–6.

1902–03
Hibernian (Cathkin), 0–0.
Hibernian (Edinburgh), 5–0.
Final.
St. Mirren (Ibrox), 5–2.

1903–04
Queen's Park (Cathkin), 2–1.
Final.
Rangers (Hampden), 2–5.

1904–05
Queen's Park (Cathkin), 3–0.
Final.
Partick Thistle (Ibrox), 2–0.

1905–06
Rangers (Hampden), 3–5.

1906–07
Queen's Park (Cathkin), 6–2.
Final.
Rangers (Cathkin), 0–1.

1907–08
Partick Thistle (Celtic Park), 3–2.
Final.
Clyde (Celtic Park), 2–0.

1908–09
Clyde (Celtic Park), 2–1.
Final.
Rangers (Celtic Park), 2–4.

1909–10
Third Lanark (Cathkin), 0–1.

1910–11
Third Lanark (Celtic Park), 5–2.
Final.
Rangers (Hampden), 1–2.

1911–12
Partick Thistle (Firhill), 5 corners to 2 corners.
Final.
Clyde (Hampden), 7 corners to 0.

1912–13
Clyde (Celtic Park), 1–0.
Third Lanark (Cathkin), 2–1.
Final.
Rangers (Celtic Park), 3–2.

1913–14
Queen's Park (Hampden), 3–0.
Final.
Third Lanark (Hampden), 6–0.

1914–15
Queen's Park (Hampden), 2–1.
Partick Thistle (Firhill), 1 goal 4 corners
   to 1 goal 3 corners.
Final.
Rangers (Ibrox), 3–2.

1915–16
Rangers (Celtic Park), 3–0.
Final.
Partick Thistle (Hampden), 2–0.

1916–17
Rangers (Ibrox), 2–0.
Final.
Queen's Park (Hampden), 1–0.

1917–18
Third Lanark (Hampden), 2–1.
Final.
Partick Thistle (Hampden), 2–0.

1918–19
Queen's Park (Hampden), 1–3.

1919–20
Rangers (Ibrox), 2–1.
Final.
Queen's Park (Hampden), 1–0.

1920–21
Partick Thistle (Celtic Park), 2–0.
Final.
Rangers (Hampden), 2–0.

1921–22
Partick Thistle (Firhill), 3 goals and 8 corners
   to 3 goals and 6 corners.
Rangers (Hampden), 6 corners to 10 corners.

1922–23
Clyde (Firhill), 1 goal 2 corners to 1 goal 1 corner.
Rangers (Celtic Park), 0–1.

1923–24
Queen's Park (Hampden), 2–0.
Final.
Rangers (Hampden), 2–1.

1924–25
Partick Thistle (Celtic Park), 1–2.

1925–26
Partick Thistle (Firhill), 2–1.
Third Lanark (Celtic Park), 2–0.
Final.
Queen's Park (Ibrox), 2–1.

1926–27
Rangers (Celtic Park), 1–4.

1927–28
Rangers (Celtic Park), 0–2.

1928–29
Queen's Park (Hampden), 6–5.
Clyde (Hampden), 3–1.
Final.
Rangers (Ibrox), 2–4.

1929–30
Queen's Park (Hampden), 4–1.
Clyde (Celtic Park), 1–0.
Final.
Rangers (Hampden), 2–2, Rangers won
    Cup by toss of coin.

1930–31
Rangers (Hampden), 2 goals 1 corner
    to 2 goals 3 corners.

1931–32
Partick Thistle (Firhill), 2–1.
Third Lanark (Celtic Park), 1–2.

1932–33
Clyde (Celtic Park), 3–1.
Queen's Park (Hampden), 2–3.

1933–34
Clyde (Celtic Park), 2–1.
Third Lanark (Hampden), 4–1.
Final.
Rangers (Hampden), 0–1.

1934–35
Queen's Park (Celtic Park), 1–4.

1935–36
Partick Thistle (Celtic Park), 1–0.
Final.
Rangers (Hampden), 4–2.

1936–37
Clyde (Celtic Park), 3–1.
Final.
Queen's Park (Hampden), 4–3.

1937–38
Queen's Park (Hampden), 3–1.
Partick Thistle (Celtic Park), 3–2.
Final.
Rangers (Hampden), 2–0.

1938–39
Clyde (Celtic Park), 2–3.